# HOW TO READ
# PATTERN

# HOW TO READ
# PATTERN

*A crash course in textile design*

HERBERT PRESS
LONDON

Clive Edwards

HERBERT PRESS

An imprint of A&C Black Publishers Limited

36 Soho Square

London W1D 3QY, UK

www.acblack.com

This book was created by

**Ivy Press**

210 High Street

Lewes, East Sussex BN7 2NS, UK

First published in 2009

ISBN: 978-1-4081-0943-4

CREATIVE DIRECTOR Peter Bridgewater

PUBLISHER Jason Hook

EDITORIAL DIRECTOR Caroline Earle

ART DIRECTOR Michael Whitehead

CONSULTANT EDITOR Simon Seivewright

PROJECT EDITOR Sanaz Nazemi

CONCEPT DESIGN Alan Osbahr

DESIGN JC Lanaway

PICTURE RESEARCH Katie Greenwood

Printed in China

# CONTENTS

Introduction 6

**How Pattern Works** 10
**Natural World** 38
**Flora** 58
**Fauna** 82
**Stylised** 104
**Geometric** 126
**Abstract** 146
**Objects** 166
**Grids & Stripes** 184
**Human Figure** 204
**Conversational** 224

Glossary 246
Resources 251
Index 252
Acknowledgements 256

# INTROD

From simple, two-colour checks such as gingham, to complex, multi-coloured repeating patterns with intricate designs representing historical events; from plain weave to velvet; and from single, embroidered masterpieces to mass-produced prints, textile patterns have been an essential feature of dress and decoration historically and remain so today. Whether we look at them in museums and galleries, wear them daily or for special occasions, or use them to decorate our homes and buildings, we are in contact with textiles of various sorts all the time. Textiles have a language of their own and any appreciation of them is enhanced by a knowledge of the vocabulary being used, the symbolism and imagery employed by the designer, and the techniques that went into their crafting and construction. A number of systems may be used in trying to classify this language. Analysis of pattern is often broken down into four broad categories: floral, geometric, abstract and conversational (or pictorial). In this book we have divided the world of pattern into ten major sections that more accurately reflect the vast range of designs. In each, the reader will be introduced to the magic of textile patterns and the vast array of different influences that have informed them. Influences include geography, technology, politics, history, invention, fashion and symbolism, as well as other art and design movements associated with the period of production.

The first section of this book is an introduction to the materials, techniques and usage of patterned textiles. This is followed by a section on patterns related to the natural world in general. A look at more specific developments in terms of flora and fauna follows this. Later sections cover stylised, geometric and abstract patterns, the depiction of objects from everyday life, grids and stripes, and imagery derived from the human figure. Finally, patterns that might set you thinking or talking about their designs (that is, conversational patterns) are examined. This book is both a reference work and something to enjoy. So try looking at patterns more closely and let the world of pattern surprise you.

# Looking for Clues

There are a number of clues to use in unravelling the mysteries of any patterned fabric. A good starting point is the textile itself. How was it produced? The method of production, weaving, printing, embroidery and lace-making each contribute their own effect to the final pattern. What colours and dyestuffs were used? Is the fabric to be used for furnishing, clothing or carpets? Is it for everyday use or for special occasions? Finally, what sort of pattern or motif does it bear? This last question is key, as an understanding of the elements of pattern and the particular shapes and motifs that are used will significantly develop your appreciation of pattern and design.

### Natural forms
Most cultures produce patterns featuring forms taken from nature, but familiarity with a range of variations will enable you to refine the possible origins and identify a range of styles, from Japanese bamboo leaves to Art Nouveau poppies, with confidence.

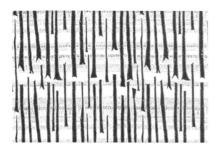

## Abstraction

A forest of trees or a set of abstract lines? Sometimes a pattern is in the eye of the beholder. Abstraction frees up the imagination to look at the possibilities.

## Geometry

Many of the oldest patterns have a geometrical base and although more modern treatments may mix the forms up a little, even a short examination will reveal circles, triangles and rectangles as key shapes in this example.

## Cultural associations

Some patterns have an immediate connection with the country or culture that produced them. Tartan instantly evokes Scotland, elaborate calligraphic devices recall Islamic pattern culture, and complex, woven knotwork has links with Celtic motifs.

## Symbolism

A motif may have been chosen for a reason that goes beyond its mere appearance. Is this lively piece a treatment of a fruiting orchard or does it have a deeper significance? Some knowledge of its context will help you to 'place' it and read any extra meanings that the designer intended.

# Introduction

The main methods to create pattern on or in textiles are weaving, printing, tapestry work, embroidery and lace work. The weaving process uses a loom, so that pattern size is determined by the width of the loom and is noted as full-width, half, quarter, etc. In printing, the processes allow for a range of patterns, dependent on the method being used. In tapestry work there is great scope for producing very complex design (one of the reasons tapestries are often pictorial). The same may be said for embroidery and lace work, in which the patterns can also be as complex as desired, but are usually created on a much smaller scale.

**Tapestry, detail, France, c.1475–90**
This wool and silk piece from Tournai depicts the story of the Trojan War. Warriors in 15th-century armour and nobles in rich costumes, alongside a magnificent tent, vividly demonstrate the level of fine pictorial detail that tapestry can achieve.

**Cotton, England, c.1830–40**
The taste for the Romantic imagery of medieval times – popular for interiors from the early to the mid 19th century is reflected in this elaborate design featuring Gothic windows. The simple half-drop repeat on this printed furnishing fabric makes the pictorial design look even more complex.

**Satin and silk, India, c.1850**

Finely embroidered in chain stitch with silks, this skirt length depicts delicate floral leaf designs with a floral border at the hem. The ground colour is characteristic of Gujarati/Kutch embroidery, but the floral motifs have obviously been inspired by Mughal designs.

**Cotton, England, 1891**

A daffodil block-printed furnishing fabric designed by John Henry Dearle, head designer for Morris & Co. His style epitomises the Arts and Crafts approach that employs naturalistic imagery, but here he has combined it with elements of either Turkish or Persian geometric design.

**Silk, England, 1971**

A screenprinted chiffon dress fabric designed by Zandra Rhodes shows the influence of the pop/hippy culture of its time. The fascination with the 'flower power' of the period is evident in the stylised blooms with button centres, rendered in a childlike naive style.

# Techniques: Weaving

There are three main categories of weave that produce pattern. These are simple (also known as plain or tabby), dobby and complex weaves. Simple or tabby weave uses a system in which each weft passes over one warp and under the next to create a balanced criss-cross effect. By altering the colours of the warps or wefts, stripes are created, and if both the warps and wefts are changed, the finished weave will be checked. The dobby system raises the warp thread in some areas to create a design, usually a small-scale geometric pattern. Compound weaves, such as damask or brocatelle, are usually made with a Jacquard mechanism that drives the patterning effect. A simple base weave with extra yarns for loop or pile creates velvet cords.

**Silk, France, c.1700**
This expensive damask used for a dress is brocaded in coloured silks and silver-gilt thread. Its design features seed pods and flower heads in two regular repeating columns along the length of the cloth. The particular pattern, and colour combination, date its creation to the beginning of the 18th century.

**Sample book, England, early 18th century**
These pages in pencil, watercolour and
body colour give an idea of how a designer
worked. Patterns for production were
usually prepared on paper for the weaver
to interpret. These designs are typical of
the lively floral styles of the time.

**Velvet, Italy, 19th century**
The weaving of velvet requires the pile
yarns to be woven over wires; the wires
are removed after a loop is made and
the pile is cut evenly. In this example, the
crown motif is supported by symmetrical
arabesques with abstract curves and
stylised leaves and branches.

**Silk, detail, England, 1850–80**
This fragment shows a stylised paisley
motif. This design features in many textiles
and is based on a droplet-shaped vegetal
motif of Persian origin. In the Persian
language the shape is called a *boteh*
(*see pages 114–15*). Other names for this
particular shape include pear and pine cone.

**Silk, England, 1862**
A Jacquard-woven
furnishing fabric called
'Raphael' manufactured
by Daniel Waters & Sons,
for the 1862 London
International Exhibition.
The Jacquard mechanism
enables each warp yarn
to be lifted separately,
which allows beautiful
and highly intricate
patterns to be woven.

# Techniques: Printing

There are four primary types of printing process. Direct printing uses blocks or relief rollers to print the cloth. Blocks usually measure up to 41cm (16in.) maximum, whilst rollers are generally limited to a 56cm (22in.) repeat height. Flat-plate intaglio printing was later superseded by roller printing – although both can create fine lines and subtle shading. Screenprinting is a form of stencilling. Screens offer a barrier to the colourant, so multicolour prints are easily made using multiplier screens. There are no limits to the height of a pattern screenprinted by hand, but the machine method normally limits repeats to a maximum of 1 metre (3⅓ft.).

**Cotton, England, c.1770s**

A printed bed-hanging in a fabric made by Nixon and Co., using the copperplate printing process. The method created fine detail and delicate rendering that had not been previously possible. It also allowed for much bigger pattern repeats, which created textiles ideal for curtains and bed-hangings.

**Cotton, England, 1888**

This block-printed cotton with a winding repeat of stylised leaves was designed in 1888 by Lewis Foreman Day. Although rather derivative of previous patterns, its twirling, repeating pattern is characteristic of many popular Arts and Crafts textiles dating from the late 19th century.

**Cotton, England, c.1923**

Designed by Minnie McLeish for William Foxton, this Art Deco furnishing fabric was shown at the Paris Exhibition in 1925. Its large-scale flowers and butterflies give it a vibrant charm and reflect the influence of late 17th-century English textiles.

**Cotton, detail, England, 1934**

Designed by Czechoslovak-born Reco Capey, this woodblock-printed cloth was made into a curtain exhibited by the Arts and Crafts Exhibition Society. Flowers and leaves are printed in the muted colours often associated with the interior decoration of the Art Deco period.

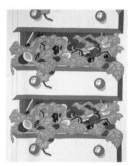

**Cotton, England, 19/3**

Named 'Salad Days', the pattern bursting out from this screenprinted furnishing textile was designed by Kay Politowicz for Textra Fabrics. The repeat is created by an amusing juxtaposition of unexpected and contrasting elements.

# Techniques: Tapestry

Tapestry weave is a version of a weft-faced textile in which the wefts do not necessarily extend across the full width of the cloth. In fact, the pattern is built up from weft threads inserted as required. The weft thus completely covers the warp, so the textile is reversible. The technique is very versatile and has been used to create patterned and pictorial clothes, carpets, rugs and hangings. Although tapestry is an ancient technique, its association today is almost invariably with woven wall hangings, which means that some other forms, also technically 'tapestries', such as heavyweight geometric kelims or delicate Chinese silk *kesi* work have become less familiar, despite the fact that their designs are often of astonishing beauty.

**Tapestry, southern Netherlands or Flanders, c.1476–1510**
The story of Susanna and the Elders is featured in this piece, which is also bordered with the coats of arms of the Gossenbrot, Relinser and Welser families. Scrolling leafwork and birds used in the borders are found only in tapestries commissioned by German patrons at this date.

**Tapestry, detail, Belgium, late 15th century**
The famous Tournai tapestry depicts the Trojan War and is full of beautifully executed and lively scenes of battle, kings, queens, warriors and horses. Here we see King Priam and his nobles in contemporary costume at the gates of Troy.

**Tapestry, Italy, c.1560**
Made in Florence, this wool and silk piece shows 'Manhood', from the series *The Life of Man*. Tapestries were often produced in series, each panel the chapter in a story. In many cases famous artists drew cartoons for the weavers to work from.

**Tapestry, England, c.1600–10**
A silk and wool cushion cover by the Sheldon tapestry workshops, depicts the return of the Prodigal Son. Although based on a Flemish design, the naïvety and bright colours of this pattern design distinguish it as English.

**Tapestry, England, 1900**
This wool and silk panel woven onto a cotton warp depicts Pomona, goddess of the orchard. Designed by the eminent artist Edward Burne-Jones and woven in the William Morris workshop, it epitomises the Arts and Crafts approach to design, in its combined use of both mythology and naturalism.

# Techniques: Embroidery

Embroidery is a patterning process that is simple in principle and very versatile. It is based on an enormous variety of stitches, but there are four basic techniques: laid or couched work, raised work, flat running and filling stitches, and counted thread work. The choice of stitch will determine the outcome of the pattern; so, for example, satin stitch will fill an area, while running stitch or couching will outline a shape. Crewel work is a style of free embroidery that does not directly follow the base threads. Because embroidery has the ability to create curvilinear shapes, it is useful for small-scale detailed embellishment and can result in patterns of exquisite delicacy.

**Linen canvas, England, c.1570–85**
The Oxburgh hanging was made by Mary, Queen of Scots and her ladies during her imprisonment by Elizabeth I. Most of the motifs of sea creatures and ships were copied from the woodcut illustrations of emblem books and natural histories that were highly personal to the queen.

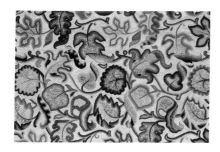

**Linen and cotton, England, c.1660–1700**
A crewel-work curtain embroidered with crewel wools of a type very popular over the period 1660–1720. These designs were influenced by contemporary Indian embroidered, printed and painted textiles that were imported into Europe by the East India Company.

**Wool, England, c.1700–50**
The light and delicate floral pattern on this wool-on-wool embroidered curtain reflects its debt to the rococo style – lightweight, decorative, frivolous and asymmetrical. Although stylised, the flowers in this pattern remain recognisable.

**Linen, detail, Greece, 18th century**
This silk-embroidered tapering panel from Kos is part of a curtain designed to hang around a bed like a tent, known as a *sperveri*. The pattern is made up from a vertical row of lozenges with a straightforward border of single stars.

**Silk, India, 19th century**
This satin-weave textile is exquisitely embroidered with silk thread in the shape of a wheel or web and comes from the northern region of Kutch. The chariot wheel is the symbol of Surya, the Hindu god of the sun.

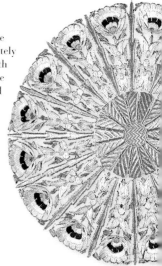

# Techniques: Lace

First made in Italy and Flanders, lace is an openwork net textile often worked in linen and generally defined in four categories: embroidered, needlepoint, bobbin (pillow) or machine lace. Embroidered lace is based on a number of patterning techniques, including cutwork, drawn and pulled threads, knotted nets (*filet*) and darned net technique (*burato*). Needlepoint patterns are worked with a single thread and needle using buttonhole stitch, thus resembling embroidery work. Bobbin or pillow lace patterns are made from many threads wound on bobbins and twisted together in different ways, while being held taut by pins.

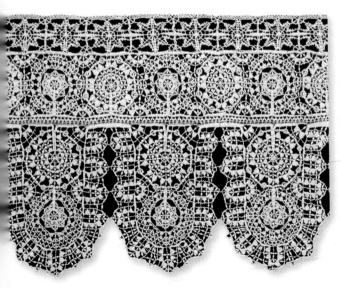

**Lace border, Italy, c.1630–40**
A bobbin lace border featuring pendant sections containing roundels shaped like wheels. The strips across the top feature eight-pointed stars in various shapes, which are also found in the roundels. These probably reflect the method of making, rather than any attempt at symbolism.

**Lace, Flanders, c.1725–50**
This very busy pattern of bobbin lace, made in Brussels, has a castle-like building at its centre, surrounded by flowers, birds and figures. The complex imagery, which was time-consuming to produce, made such panels expensive accessories for the wealthy of the time.

**Lace, Belgium c.1850s**
A highly fashionable veil or shawl combining both needle lace and bobbin lace motifs. Featuring garlands around the perimeter with stylised ferns and flowers in bouquets and groups, it demonstrates the taste for lavish floral designs in the mid 19th century.

**Lace, Belgium, c.1860–70**
Applied to machine net, this mixed needle and bobbin lace design makes a very delicate flounce, intended as a dress trimming. The repeated scrolls, fronds and pineapple motif seem to reflect the rococo revival of the mid to late 19th century.

**Lace, Germany, 1884**
In the late 19th century, middle-class taste for peasant-style lace developed in conjunction with rural regeneration schemes. The Erzgebirge region of Saxony and Bohemia was encouraged to make *torchon* lace. The naïvety of the tree design reflects the peasant style.

# Techniques: Rug weaving

Rug or carpet weaving can be undertaken in a variety of ways, but the best-known process is the tying of a series of knots onto a warp with a binding weft. These so-called 'oriental' carpets or rugs are patterned in innumerable ways, often dependent upon the region where they are produced. Knotted rugs have been made all over the world. In the case of Middle Eastern and Far Eastern work, the patterns often include symbols and motifs that can readily be interpreted and which, in their originating cultures, will be almost universally understood, whilst European patterns are often more purely pictorial.

**Carpet, Iran, late 16th–early 17th century**
Noteworthy not only for its border with a white background, but also for the animated representation of the animals amongst the floral designs, this Safavid piece, with a wool pile on a silk warp and weft, is of extremely high quality.

**Carpet, Transylvania, 17th century**
Hand-knotting sometimes creates interesting asymmetric effects, as the maker tries to shoehorn an entire pattern into limited space. In this example, knotted in wool on a cotton warp and weft, there has been insufficient space to complete a cartouche in the upper right-hand corner of the border.

**Carpet, detail,
England, 1889**

This richly coloured
and complex design
by William Morris
consists of scrolling
arabesques with
stylised flowers and
birds. The effect is
symmetrical, but
viewed closely,
there are subtle
differences in the
mirror patterning.

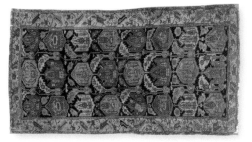

**Carpet, detail, Persia, 17th century**

The designer has used two lattices of
different sizes, slightly offset to create a
regularly repeating structure of flowers and
leaves. These designs were later copied for
machine production, although this example
is hand-knotted in wool and silk.

**Carpet, Caucasia, 19th century**

A hand-knotted woollen pile on woollen
warp and weft, this piece has two very
similar motifs. There are two different
frames for the inner motifs, which are
themselves framed by stylised palm
fronds. The whole is enclosed by a
symmetrical border.

# Techniques: Dyeing

**Textile fragment mounted in an album, Japan, 19th century**
By drawing a pattern on the cloth with rice paste extruded through a metal tip fixed to a cloth bag, the maker creates a coat that stops the colour penetrating when the dyes are applied – the resist-dye technique – thereby creating the pattern.

In pattern-making terms, dyeing only selected parts of a cloth is a worldwide method and the techniques used are many and various. These techniques include tie and dye, stitch resist, starch or wax resist, and ikat. The resist-dyeing systems apply a barrier to parts of the cloth so that a pattern is only produced on the unmarked or tied parts. Mordants, such as alum, create a chemical link between dyes that would otherwise be fugitive and the cloth to which they are applied, to make colourfast patterns. Historically, mordants have included salt, vinegar, citrus juice and lye.

**Cotton, England, 1883**

'Strawberry Thief' is one of William Morris's most famous designs. The indigo discharge and block-print pattern was based on the thrushes which often stole strawberries from the kitchen garden of Morris's Oxfordshire home, Kelmscott Manor.

**Silk, detail, India, late 19th century**

This ceremonial cloth or *patolu* with an elephant-and-tiger design was created for export to the Indonesian market. This kind of woven silk was a specialism of Gujarati weavers, who used a highly refined resist-dyed double ikat technique.

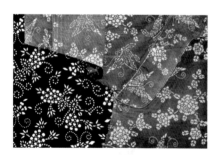

**Cotton, China, c.1880–1950, and 20th century**

The jacket and the textile length shown together here demonstrate the ikat process of tying yarns to create patterns, known in Japan as *kasuri*. Such designs are often minimalist, abstract or stylised – both cloths in the image here have simple, floral patterns.

**Cotton, detail, England, 1935**

A curtain made up with printed cloth produced by the discharge process, which dyes a cloth in one colour and then prints on a bleaching agent to reveal the pattern. Designed by Reco Capey, this design was shown at the Arts and Crafts Exhibition of 1935.

# Materials: Yarn

The fundamental materials that make most textiles, yarns are produced from both natural and artificial fibres. Historically, cloth was woven from wool, linen, silk and cotton yarns, but in the 20th century science added synthetics such as polyester, nylon and rayon. The various yarns have different properties that affect the final look of the pattern in the cloth. Silk is soft with a luxurious sheen; cotton is strong, smooth and fine, and so takes dyes very well; wool is hard-wearing and equally at home as a floor covering or made up into a coat; and linen has traditionally as a base for embroidery work.

**Wool, England, c.1845–50**
Part of a set of woven church furnishings designed by A.W.N. Pugin for use in St Augustine's Church, which was built in the grounds of Pugin's own house in Ramsgate, Kent. The pattern, based on a small, repeating medallion with a crown, has a monogram in a Gothic style of lettering.

### Silk and wool, England, 1879

Designed by William Morris, this green, cream and blue hand-loom Jacquard-woven curtain encompasses a design entitled 'Flower Garden'. The cross-section of formal repeating flower heads was used in several other contemporary Morris products. The colours were suggested by inlaid metals seen by Morris.

### Linen, England, 1931

Linen has a long pedigree in furnishings, amongst many other uses. It takes dyes well and is often used as a base cloth for printing. This furnishing fabric, designed by Gregory Brown for William Foxton, features a windmill and a forester wielding an axe, and the fluid curves give the pattern an animated quality.

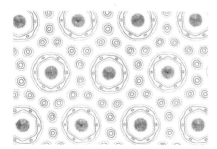

### Cotton, England, 1951

A printed cotton entitled 'Haemoglobin', a design from the Festival of Britain Pattern Group, inspired by the scientific images of crystal structures recording the arrangement of atoms in various substances. The repetitive symmetry and regularity of the images proved ideal for fabric repeats.

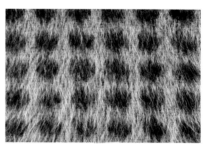

### Mohair, wool and nylon, England, 1957

A two-colour fabric sample woven from three fibres, this mohair example features a fluffy-edged grey and black check. On the back of the fabric the colours are reversed. Unusual yarn types can be used to lend their own qualities to even the simplest patterns.

# Elements: Colour

Although patterns can work well in monochrome, the addition of colour is often vitally important in defining designs. Colours follow fashion, have an influence on our psyche, have symbolic value and express style. Colour may be used to try to imitate nature or to surprise the eye by doing exactly the opposite; it may also carry political, religious or military associations. Colour and pattern are combined to express human emotions and ideas, as well as to straightforwardly depict images of our surroundings. From simple tone on tone to outrageously psychedelic or vibrant mixes, colour is the key complement to pattern.

**Silk, fragment, China, 16th–18th century**
A woven damask in blue and yellow with a pattern of scrolling flower heads and linking foliage. In China, yellow was considered to be the colour of the emperor, as he stood at the centre of the universe like the sun.

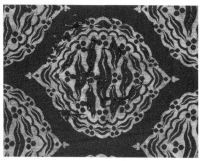

**Silk, Turkey, 17th century**
Anzogee-shaped repeating motif on damask textile. The pale pink on deep red makes a very effective colour contrast. This hue stands for beauty, grace and goodness and has traditionally been associated with marriage and sensuality.

**Silk, France, c.1760–64**
Patterns from sample books remain unfaded so often give a better idea of the original colour than materials that have been used. This French example has a vivid pink background with neoclassical stylised leaves and other motifs in overlaid gold.

**Wool, detail, Algeria, late 19th century**
Part of an applied pattern on a man's hooded jacket: the star shapes and associated linking patterns are prepared from cut pieces and appliquéd in a rainbow of colours. The unsophisticated nature of the stitching gives the piece the simple, straightforward quality characteristic of 'ethnic' work.

**Textile sample book, Japan, 1938**
This motif of bamboo leaves on a fretted background was designed for use on silk or synthetics. The violet colour gives the pattern a cooler, calmer quality, tempering the strong blaze of red.

# Elements: Motif

Pattern is very much part of the language of textiles, and motifs are the words and letters of that language. Like language, too, patterns derive from numerous cultures from the past and are recycled over many centuries. The symbols and motifs that have originally been important to a particular culture are then used in new contexts and lose that significance, but may perhaps gain another one. Pattern motifs may be divided into three main categories: floral, geometric and conversational, and then subdivided into many more. Within these general groups there are many hundreds of motifs that may be applied to textiles.

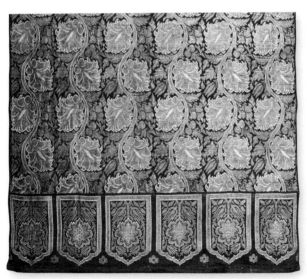

**Silk, Turkey, c.1700–29**
A woven cushion cover with a stylised and regularly repeating plant motif in gold and white on a deep-red ground. The shield shapes at the end of the pattern create a border that will appear at one end of the cushion.

**Cotton, India, c.1740–60**

The pattern of flowers and a bird on this fabric is so delicately embroidered that it might be mistaken for a printed design. The piece is a typical example of the superb chain-stitch work done in Gujarat, using both a tambour hook and a needle. It was made as a dress material, for the export market in England.

**Silk, Pakistan, early 20th century**

A skirt length made in Sindh from silk embroidered with silk in a chain stitch. The motif of a small paisley or *boteh* design is typical of its area of origin. It is quite common for *botehs* to decorate the entire field as a repetitive all-over pattern, as shown here.

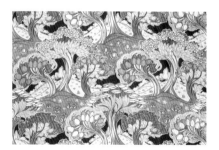

**Cotton, England, 1902**

This roller-printed furnishing fabric by F. Steiner & Co. has a brightly coloured design of swirling trees, characteristic of the vibrant and sinuous Art Nouveau 'whiplash' motif. This particular motif which is found in many items – both textiles and objects – that were designed in the early 20th century.

**Cotton, England, 1935**

Dress fabrics with floating motifs on a plain ground, like this crêpe, were particularly fashionable in the 1930s. The apparently random repeat effect and the freedom of line and form that rejected naturalistic copying reflect contemporary artistic movements and an informal approach to design.

# Use: Apparel

Textiles are an ubiquitous part of clothing and apparel. Clothing may be for everyday use or for special occasions; it may range from mass-produced to designer limited edition. The range of materials used is enormous, as is the choice of patterns that have been employed. In many cases the degree and quality of the pattern-making express the status of the wearer, although there have been numerous attempts at imitating luxury effects inexpensively. Particular patterns are sometimes associated with specific types of garment, such as saris, shawls and kimonos.

**Silk, satin and linen, France, c.1670–90**
Image robes were used to dress religious statues. This example is decorated with straw plaits couched with yellow silk, forming a design consisting of scrolls, themselves making ogee-shaped compartments, each of which encloses a fleur-de-lys. The use of straw was intentional and may symbolically refer to the blessing of the harvest.

**Silk velvet, England, early 18th century**
The tabard was a ceremonial garment bearing armorial devices worn by a herald. The front, back and arms of this example, richly embroidered in silver-gilt and silver thread, bear the royal arms in use between 1714 and 1801, representing England, Scotland, France, Ireland and Brunswick.

**Silk, France, c.1715**
This luxurious silk damask with supplementary patterning wefts, with its lively pattern and distinct colouring, represents the height of fashion at the time. Contact between Asia and Europe influenced the design of fashionable silks such as this.

**Cotton, England, 1934**
The lively jigging sailor and seagull motifs on this roller-printed dress fabric are heavily stylised, and the striking colouring may have been influenced by graphic designs and the advertising motifs of the 1930s, which often used sharp-edged triangular imagery.

**Paper, England, 1967**
A disposable mini-dress made from a washable bonded cellulose fibre. This striking print of large green swirls in a symmetrical pattern was based on an Art Nouveau design that was also used for furnishing fabric. There was a revival during the 1960s of Art Nouveau imagery, often applied with a contemporary Pop Art spin.

# Use: Furnishing

Like clothes, textile furnishings have a long and complex history. Also in the same way as garments, furnishings may be humble, extravagant, or somewhere in between. Whatever their use, they will often be patterned. Furnishing textiles have been made with all sorts of designs, some being aimed at and subsequently identified with particular kinds of space. For example, chintzes are often equated with cosy cottage interiors; ginghams with a log-cabin. Frontier-living style; and damasks with luxurious drawing rooms.

**Cotton, Greece, 18th century**

A woven and embroidered bed tent from Rhodes with large flower-motif panels, leaves, peacocks and a six-point star, in old gold, red and green with blue detailing, on a cream ground. In this case the patterning is probably simply decorative, with no intended symbolism. The neat, stylised rows of formal motifs are characteristic of much European folk art, from textiles to ceramics.

**Designs for carpets, Britain, c.1850**
Intended for the Houses of Parliament these carpet designs, by A.W.N. Pugin, clearly reflect his interest in medieval encaustic tiles and the geometry of pattern. The idea of a tile design reproduced in carpet would have appealed to the mid 19th-century design reformers.

**Cotton, England, 1883**
'Wey', an indigo-discharge block-printed furnishing fabric by William Morris. To create this pattern, cotton was first put into indigo dye. On removal it oxidised to produce the blue colour, and was then block-printed with bleach, so that the final print featured dark blue, pale blue and white.

**Wool, Holland, c.1915–20**
A table cover of woven plush featuring a design formed by an elongated shield-shaped panel. The motif reflects the artistic interest in so-called 'primitive art' and the abstract elements found in objects such as African carvings that was prevalent at the beginning of the 20th century.

**Silk, France, 1921**
Fashion illustrator Georges Barbier designed this sample, called *Venise fête de nuit*. It shows romantic scenes of revellers playing musical instruments on board gondolas, with the buildings of Venice subtly reflected in woven 'shadows' in the canal.

# Use: Specialised

Although textiles are most widely used for clothing and furnishings, they have always also had a wide variety of other specialised applications. These range from ceremonial textiles to bags and flags. The decorative value of textiles has meant that they can be used to indicate something unique and special as well as in more mundane objects. Many worked textiles, such as embroidery, needlework and lace have been produced as craftwork intended to display their maker's virtuosity.

**Velvet, England and Italy, c.1470–1500** Woven in Italy and embroidered in England, this altar frontal with applied embroidery on linen uses silver-gilt thread and coloured silks to embellish the pattern. Occasionally, as depicted here, representations of the figures of the donors are included in the design, and can be identified by their meticulously embroidered names.

## Linen, England, c.1540

The Calthorpe purse is finely embroidered with silk in tent stitch and shows how heraldic devices are used to declare possession and ancestry. The heraldry also displays four marriage connections and reflects the importance of family pedigree to its owner.

## Linen, Spain, 18th century

Samplers showed 'samples' of patterns and stitches and afforded instruction and practice for girls in the art of needlework. This example is densely worked with geometric patterns and lifelike decoration in a variety of stitches that exhibits the range of the maker's skills.

## Silk, Italy, mid 18th century

A luxurious embroidered chalice veil, worked with coloured silks and metal thread on a cream ground. During the Eucharist a veil is often used to cover the chalice and paten to prevent any contact being made with the bread and wine; it is also intended to honour the vessel used for the sacrament.

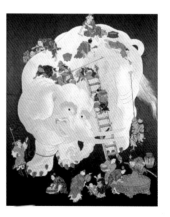

## Silk, Japan, c.1800–50

A gift cover or *fukusa* made from embroidered satin, mounted on scarlet crêpe, a white elephant – this silk features the motif of being washed by 18 men who use a ladder to reach the animal's back. It symbolises both strenght of mind and vanity.

# Introduction

Throughout the ages, designers have taken inspiration for pattern-making directly from their natural surroundings. Natural forms offer a treasure trove of imagery that can be copied directly, stylised into recognisable shapes or abstracted to the point at which the inspiration for the pattern is only just discernible. The range of images adapted to patterns is vast, but particular forms recur all through textile history. Leaves, trees, plants in various guises and fruit have all been employed in the service of pattern-making. In many cases, the particular species or style chosen has symbolic significance.

**Velvet, fragment, Italy, c.1370–1400**
This small portion of brocaded silk velvet has a pattern of sprigs of trailing, wisteria-like flowers produced in cut pile. The brocading process enables parts of the pattern to be raised and made prominent.

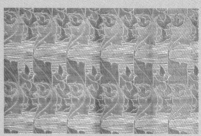

**Cotton, England, c.1780–1810**

A block-printed furnishing fabric which, although it was produced in England, clearly references the hand-painted Indian patterns that inspired it. A mix of strong vertical elements is countered by the dainty infill, with a visible repeat.

**Silk and wool, England, c.1900**

'Bird and Leaf' is the name of this pattern on a woven double-cloth intended for furnishing and designed by C.F.A. Voysey, who influenced Art Nouveau design. His work at this period featured regular, symmetrical repeats of flowing patterns that might incorporate pastel-shaded birds, animals, hearts, flowers or trees in silhouette.

**Rayon, England c.1946**

Entitled 'Jungle', this furnishing material was designed by the artist Felix Topolski for Ascher Ltd, London, a company well known for producing fabrics designed by fine artists. Artists enjoyed working with the screenprinting process as used on this fabric, because it was possible to create larger, more complex patterns than rollers.

**Cotton, England, 1950**

Made for furnishing fabric, this poppy-scattered pattern was named 'Britomart' by its designer, Sylvia Priestley. The name has multiple applications: Britomartis is a nymph in Greek mythology, while Britomart is a character in both Spenser's *The Faerie Queene* and Shaw's *Major Barbara*.

# Leaves

### Ancient to Modern

Leaves are one of the most prevalent motifs and their symbolism is common to many cultures. Ivy leaves are often used to signify strong and enduring friendship: the association comes from their ability to cling to a surface even in difficult situations. Oak leaves symbolise faith and endurance, and bay leaves were traditionally thought to be an antidote for poison and were therefore used to symbolise healing. In Buddhist culture the *bodhi* (Asian fig) leaf, which has a heart-shaped profile, has symbolic associations with love. Generally, when leaves are bunched they represent group action and solidity of purpose, whereas the single leaf is an ancient heraldic symbol said to signify happiness.

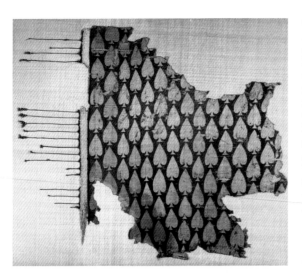

### Silk, Egypt, c.500–700

A woven textile with a decoration of lance-headed leaves in white on a brown ground, found at a burial site in Akhmim, Egypt. Such textiles were woven on looms that produced repeating patterns using a compound twill weave. The partially surviving fringe suggests that this may have been a cushion cover.

**Velvet, Italy, 16th century**

A naturalistic pattern of leaves
and flowers in pale green on an
olive-green ground gives this
velvet a sumptuous quality.
The rows of sprigs appear in
lines across and down the cloth.

**Silk, Italy, 17th century**

Woven with a pattern of
stylised flowers and fern fronds
with repeating cross shapes, this
pattern was made as a border.
This type of design was often
made up from elements selected
from standard pattern books,
but then put together in a
fresh combination.

# Leaves

**Silk, England, c.1708**
A woven damask produced in Spitalfields, London offers a variation on the stylised floral designs associated with this area, and features a vertical repeating pattern with shadowy images in the background, overlaid with natural shapes.

**Cotton and linen, England, c.1700–10**
A detail from a rectangular hanging of crewel-work embroidery, which is part of a full set of bed curtains made in the early 18th century. The style of such hangings and the twining foliage of the design were based on imported Indian embroideries.

**Linen, Ottoman Empire, 19th century**
This napkin or towel is embroidered with silk and metal thread – the rows of pattern are the borders. By the 19th century, Ottoman designs began to develop into rigid and heavily stylised patterns. The original bright colours have faded.

**Sewn patchwork, Japan, 19th century**
*Kesa* (the mantles of Buddhist priests)
like this are made from patches of cloth
pieced together – the sewing is part of
the devotional process. Here the sections
of fabric have been carefully aligned
so as not to disrupt the elegant design.

**Linen, Ottoman Empire, 19th century**
The uncomplicated detailing of the leaves'
veins and jagged outlines on the border of
the towel, together with a divided square
edging, give the finished object a simple
appeal. The embroidery features metal
thread as well as silk.

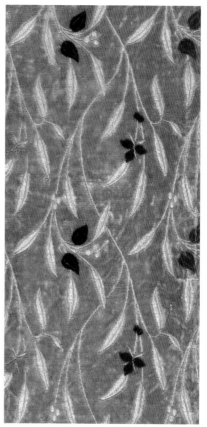

**Velvet, France, 19th century**
Aptly titled 'Golden Leaves', this attractive
fabric has a simple leaf and stem design
that trails down the warp length. Touches
of colour appear in the fruit or seed pods.
Drooping leaves make trees look graceful,
and the effect is the same here.

# Leaves

### Silk, Japan, 19th century

Wheels and leaves make up the resist-dyed decoration (*yuzen*) seen here and commonly found in Japan. The wheel is an important symbol in Buddhist and Taoist culture, representing human fate and a continual return from the circumference to the centre.

### Cotton, detail, Japan, 19th century

The stencilled decoration on a robe known as a *bingata* from the Ryukyu Islands has a background of swirling lines overlaid with maple leaves. A maple-leaf has several symbolic meanings – unity, autumn, and spiritual growth among them – and the maple tree is important in Japan and commonly depicted in textile designs.

**Lace, detail, France, 1867**
The pteridomania (fern obsession) of the mid 19th century is reflected in an example of needle lace patterned with fan fronds. This interest manifested itself in natural collections and patterns on all sorts of objects. It was ideal for demonstrating virtuosity in lace making.

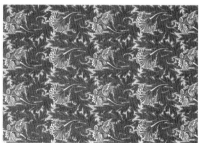

**Carpet design, England, 19th century**
The watercolour for the 'Redcar' carpet commission was designed by William Morris in 1881. It features stylised plants with an acanthus border. The colouring of the pattern, with a camel ground and pastel detailing, is typical of his early carpet designs.

**Cotton, England, 1875**
This block-printed 'Tulip' design by William Morris intended for furnishing, demonstrates Morris's interest in flat pattern. The design, with its densely floriated and repeating zigzags of waving leaves, features stylised tulips shown against a different leaf.

# Leaves

**Silk, France, early 20th century**
Aptly named '*L'Afrique*', this French patterned furnishing silk shows a taste for the exotic. It was designed by Robert Bonfils for the textile manufacturer Bianchini-Férier. During the Art Deco period French designers often used imagery from Africa, and in particluar from Egypt.

**Cotton, England, 1897**
The vertical panels of strawberries and birds that make up the repeat on this furnishing fabric would be viewed well in hanging drapery folds. It was designed by the architect C.F.A. Voysey, who was well known for his lightness of style and his confident pattern-making.

**Linen, Italy, 1927**
Mariano Fortuny, who is better known for his exquisite pleated dress fabrics, designed a pattern of cream leaf motifs and blossom shapes on a forest-green background, used on a sample of printed furnishing material. The creeping nature of the vine is captured by the pattern.

**Cotton, England, c.1905**
This woven cotton called 'Santiago' was probably designed by Archibald Knox for the Silver Studios. It features the stylised plants that were a feature of Knox's work and successfully combines Celtic and Art Nouveau elements within an Arts and Crafts tradition.

**Silk, France, c.1925–9**
'Oasis', a design by Robert Bonfils, demonstrates the use of regular pattern repeats of leaves in a muted pale-green and grey colourway. The exotic jungle look, with its reference to non-Western cultures, was a favourite Art Deco theme.

**Cotton and silk, France, c.1928**
From the late 1920s onwards, textile designs were increasingly abstract and more muted in colour. This woven damask design made up in blocks of stylised leaf patterns was produced for Betty Joel Ltd, an avant-garde interior and furniture-design business.

# Trees

### 18th–20th Century

Trees are a rich source of inspiration for the textile designer. Not only are they attractive in naturalistic representations, but as the expression of an idea they are one of the most widespread symbolic motifs. As symbols of life and growth, trees can be used to convey three levels of symbolic imagery. They have roots in the underworld; their trunks and lower branches are of the earth, and they aim for the heavens, with their upper branches reaching for the light. On a practical level, too, their vertical shapes make them ideal for many textile applications.

**Silk, detail, Japan, 19th century**

The pattern of bamboo and flowering trees on a crêpe silk (made for a Kimono) was created with a resist-dyeing technique (*yuzen*). Bamboo is believed to ward off evil influences and to bring good omens, while blossom is a symbol of purity.

### Design for silk, England, 1734

Anna Maria Garthwaite was one of the foremost English designers of the exotic textiles, later known as 'bizarre' silks, that were popular in the mid eighteenth century. This pencil and watercolour drawing shows a fanciful landscape with trees. The asymmetrical layout and sinuous curves place the pattern in the rococo style.

### Cotton, England, mid 19th century

This furnishing fabric features bridges and exotic trees and foliage in an 'island' pattern, whereby the image stands alone without any joining pattern. This may help to give a slightly more formal look to the overall patterning effect of this English textile.

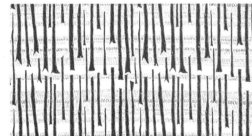

### Wool, Scotland, 1896–1900

A woven hanging, designed by the architect C.F.A. Voysey, has a pattern that was first used for wallpaper and then transferred to textiles. The design has an ethereal fairy-tale quality that would make it particularly appropriate for decorating a child's room.

### Cotton, England, 1959

Lucienne Day led the way in introducing modern abstract pattern design into the textile industry, and this roller-printed furnishing fabric called 'Forest', is a good example of her work. Designed for Heal's, its name conjures up an image which might not be read from the actual pattern.

# Trees: Specific Types

### Ancient to Modern

Designs of specific tree types are often used as textile patterns. Whether it is the palm tree from Asia, the pine tree from Japan or the English oak, most trees are decorative in themselves, as well as suggestive of symbolic value. Throughout the Far East, for example, the pine tree is considered a symbol of immortality due to its evergreen foliage and incorruptible resin. When another culture borrows symbolic imagery – as in the example of the banyan tree, below – it tends to lose its power and to become purely decorative.

**Linen, Egypt, 300–500**
This large wool embroidered hanging has a design that is in the late Egyptian classical style, with motifs from the preferred range of designs, including trees and flowers. The top border, embroidered with vines, grapes and baskets, represents nature's gifts and her fruitfulness.

**Silk, England, 18th century**
A pink brocaded silk entitled 'Banyan'. Although the banyan tree is considered sacred in the Hindu religion and represents eternal life because of its vast spreading branches, in this English usage it becomes simply an attractive sinuous pattern without special meaning.

**Cotton, India, 18th century**
A hand-painted and printed chintz
*palampore* or bed cover/hanging, with
a design of crossed palm trees, is made on
the Coromandel Coast. Large quantities of
these *palampores* were exported to Europe
in the 18th century.

**Silk, detail, Japan, 1850–80**
Shown on an embroidered crepe kimono
with paste-resist (*yuzen*) patterning, this
detail depicts pine trees and clouds. In
Japan pine trees are regarded as a symbol
of the life force, as well as an omen of
good fortune.

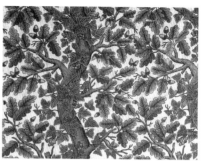

**Cotton, England, 1799**
Called 'Royal Oak and Ivy', this block-
printed fabric designed for furnishings,
is in a colour scheme known as the 'drab
style', which originated in about
1799 and was particularly
fashionable up to 1807.
The oak is a classic symbol
of strength and kingship.

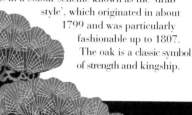

# Fruit

### 18th–20th Century

Fruit, as a classic symbol of abundance, may be represented in filled bowls or overflowing from the cornucopia or horn of plenty. Fruits have also been used to signify new beginnings, the seeds or pips offering continuity of life. Individual fruits, of course, can have their own symbolism. For example, the apple is often seen as a forbidden fruit, the pineapple symbolises hospitality and welcome, the grape is a sign of Christ in Christian iconography, and the pomegranate represents fertility. Like other natural imagery, fruit offers textile designers rich pickings.

**Silk, detail, Turkey, 18th century**

A transparent embroidered kerchief with metal thread in *musabak* and satin stitch. Although the embroidery technique is Ottoman, the pattern drawing of the grapes and leaves is more reminiscent of European botanical drawings of the mid 18th century.

**Silk and wool, England, c.1880**
A woven double cloth with a repeat of pears and cherries designed by the architect and furniture designer, Bruce J. Talbert. The pattern shows the Japanese-influenced simplicity of line that was fashionable in Britain in the late 19th century.

**Lace, detail, Belgium, late 19th century**
Taken from Brussels, flounce is made from mixed needle and bobbin lace applied to a base of machine net, this detail shows a pineapple motif – a favoured symbol of hospitality more commonly found applied to tablecloths and napkins.

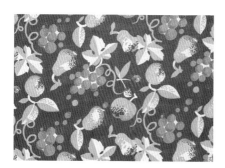

**Silk, USA, 1927**
This printed dress fabric of crêpe de Chine has a repeating fruit pattern, depicting apples and pears in citrus greens and yellows, combined with cherry and grape motifs, all shown quite naturalistically. Although individual fruits have their own particular symbolism, en masse they represent abundance.

**Linen, England, 1938**
A stylised bowl of fruit and glasses are the key features of this Art Deco design, used for a furnishing fabric. The impression is of abundance and hospitality. In some cultures the pineapple is associated with welcome. The muted colours reflect the Modernist influence on Art Deco.

# Field Flowers & Grasses

### 18th–20th Century

Among the imagery derived from natural sources, grasses and field flowers are some of the most attractive to pattern makers. The delicate stalks and seed heads allow the designer great freedom, enabling the pattern to be formal or informal, tight or loose, multi-coloured or plain. Grasses symbolise both submission and utility, and pattern-makers of the past would have been aware of this when choosing them as a subject for textile decoration. Field flowers have a delicacy that reflects a particular image of the countryside and, as such, often appear as either stylised or naturalistic motifs in many textile patterns.

**Cotton, England, late 18th century**
The technique of printing textiles with indigo to achieve colour-fast blue was developed in the 1740s. It could not be combined with other techniques, so china-blue prints were always monochrome. This plate-printed furnishing fabric used china-blue dyes to depict naturalistic feathery plants.

**Paper impression of printed textile, England, 18th–19th century**
An interesting rendering of an abstracted grass and flower scene in a monotone colouring, this example with its finely drawn imagery was produced by the print works at Bromley Hall, in East London, which were well known for their copper-plate printing.

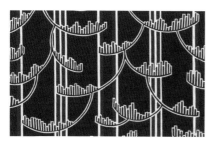

**Design for cotton, Britain, c.1840**
A watercolour and body-colour design
reflecting the trend that occurred when
the novel process of roller printing became
successful. Designers used abstract
patterns, such as this highly stylised grass
image overlaid on stripes, to meet the
demand for textiles in the new style.

**Cotton, England,
early 20th century**
Entitled 'Field
Flowers', this
furnishing fabric
was designed and
manufactured for
Liberty & Co. of
London. It was
duplex-printed,
a method whereby
the same pattern
is printed on both
sides of the fabric,
making this design
of assorted wild
flowers reversible.

**Cotton, England, early 20th century**
'Brooksby', a reversible furnishing fabric,
was designed by Liberty & Co. of London.
It features a more stylised rose pattern
than 'Field Flowers' (left) and reflects
the influence of the designs of Charles
Rennie Mackintosh.

# Tree of Life

### 18th–19th Century

The 'Tree of Life' appears in many cultures and can often be found in folklore representing immortality and/or fertility. Whether it is an evergreen tree symbolising the everlasting, or a deciduous tree that grows, loses its leaves and regrows them, symbolising regeneration, the Tree of Life is central to myths all over the world. The design was popular for chintz furnishings in Europe from the early 18th century to the start of the 19th. It was especially suited to coverlets and *palampores* (bedcovers or hangings).

**Cotton, India, c.1700**

This cut-down *palampore*, designed in south-east India for the Western market, shows a complicated and exotic flowering tree growing out of an urn of European design, and flanked by pots of flowers that have undoubtedly been taken from European prints.

**Cotton, India, 1770–80**

Typical of the styles imported into Europe in large quantities from the Coromandel Coast, this design shows a fanciful, heavily stylised tree with all sorts of flowers emanating from it. It is probable that the imagery was specially selected to appeal to a Western market.

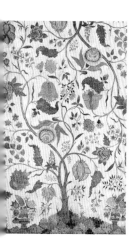

**Cotton, India, 1750–1775**
This glazed, painted and dyed cotton features Chinese influences on chintz designs for the Western market in the third quarter of the 18th century. The sinuosity of the tree and its branches are typical.

**Cotton, India, 1750–1775**
Here is a classic example of the flowering tree design, which has an extremely strong pattern that fills the central field with a branching tree and many extraordinary flowers and leaves. The curious border of a twisted stem and flowers is unusual for such designs.

**Cotton and silk, India, early 19th century**
The Tree of Life pattern embroidered in cotton and silk is the central theme of an elaborate bed coverlet. Dense with flowers and perching birds, it reaches up to touch the heavenly canopy. The symmetry of the design is stressed by two large jars of flowers positioned on the ground.

# Introduction

Flowers and floral imagery are some of the most universal patterns. They have been used widely over many centuries and in most cultures, and associated devices, such as sprigs, baskets, bouquets, wreaths and garlands have all been represented in natural, stylised or semi-abstract forms. Endlessly flexible in form, they lend themselves to large all-over spreads or small repeats, and have featured in lattices against complex grounds, spaced on light grounds, in stripes and in many other formats. Particular flowers have enjoyed fashionable favour at different times and places, and have sometimes been used for their symbolic values, too.

**Linen, detail, England, early 17th century**
Carefully placed to give a random, scattered effect, the medley of flowers delicately embroidered on this cover include thistles, cornflowers, daffodils and daisies, mixed in with the insects and even a few pears.

## Silk, Italy, late 17th century

Until recently the priest faced the altar during a service, so the back of his chasuble was, visually, the most important part. In this example, the heavily embroidered pattern is secular: images of birds and flowers mingle with a small central heraldic device.

## Silk, France, mid 18th century

The flowering tree design of this dress, on a cream ground brocaded with coloured, silver and gilt threads, would have looked spectacular when worn. The flowers are bold in their colouring, but completely un-naturalistic.

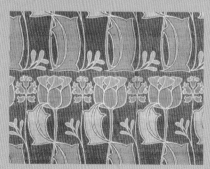

## Silk and wool, England, c.1900

Horizontal bands of pattern are the striking feature of the design shown here by Harry Napper. Large, green flowers, which are possibly stylised lotus blossoms, contrast with the bold pink leaves in two tones, creating a pattern typical of the sinuous, and forceful Art Nouveau style.

## Cotton and rayon, England, 1933

A lively Art Deco pattern of heavily abstracted flowers, this design features a repeat based around a circle that is cased in loose brushwork. This sort of design reflects the influence on commercial pattern-making of the fine-art fashions of the time.

# All-Over Pattern

### 18th–20th Century

All-over patterns cover an entire surface area leaving very little empty background, unlike those designs that rely on single or bordered motifs presented against a plain ground. It may flow in one, two or more ways, and the patterns themselves may be random or set. The one-directional type has a clear direction, usually growing from bottom to top, whereas the two-directional has motifs going both ways. Multi-directional patterns are often either regular repeats in a formal geometric relationship or seemingly random scattering which, despite its casual effect, is actually carefully planned. They are presented on textured backgrounds, such as moiré effect, as well as on plain colours.

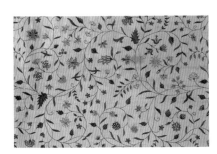

**Cotton, India, early 18th century**

A Gujarati piece embroidered with silk, is a good example of the delicate all-over 'random' designs associated with Indian work of this period. The textile has a light, informal look and the repeat is not easily evident, making it easy to match when sewing it into a finished item.

**Silk, India, mid 18th century**

Delicate flowers and leaves in a repeating sequence are embroidered on this silk hanging. Apparently informal random designs were fashionable at this period. These pieces are known as Cambay embroideries, as they were exported from the port of Cambay.

**Cotton, England, c.1850**

This fashionable printed cotton is typical of summer furnishings available in the mid 19th century. This particular design was singled out by the design reformer Henry Cole, and condemned for what he saw as its lack of symmetry and false principles of imitation.

**Cotton, England, mid 19th century**

Pilloried in 1852 in an exhibition called 'False Principles in Design', this printed and glazed chintz was condemned for its 'Direct Imitation of Nature' involving 'branches of lilac and rose trees made to bend to the forms of sofa cushions and chair arms'. As implied in the criticism, the flower forms themselves are naturalistic.

**Rayon, England, 1934**

A repeat of coloured flowers, leaves and stems on a white background gives this dress fabric a clean, fresh look. Motifs floating on a plain ground work well, and the slight abstraction of the forms may reflect the influence of contemporary fashions in fine art.

# FLORA Baskets

### 17th–19th Century

Baskets or other containers act as a focal point for displays of flowers, either as cut blooms or growing plants. The basket appears in a huge range of styles, from the literal and representational to the almost unrecognisably abstracted. The images that are included in this pattern group also cover a wide historical and geographical scope, and cross-influences can be seen in different periods and styles – for example, the Renaissance-influence on the early eighteenth-century Dutch velvet (below right).

**Silk, detail, Italy, c.1620–40**
An elaborately ornamented red stole edged with silver-gilt bobbin lace features a large cartouche in the corner, with a bowl of fruit and flowers. This depiction of tulips is particularly interesting – they had only recently arrived in Europe at the time this piece was worked.

**Carpet, detail, India, 1650**

A highly structured and formalised pattern organises two styles of vases here into a strict geometrical repeat in this high-quality hand-knotted piece from Lahore. Despite the severity of the shapes, each vase is lavishly filled with billowing flowers, ensuring that the effect is generous as well as disciplined.

**Wool, detail, Netherlands, c.1700**

The highly stylised pattern on this example features floral baskets, urns and garlands alongside some architectural elements, all derived from Renaissance designs, although the luxurious woollen velvet on which it appears was made at the beginning of the eighteenth century.

**Cotton, fragment, Ottoman Empire,
18th century**

Embroidered with silk and metal thread,
with a small repeat pattern showing gilt
dishes holding bunches of flowers and
grapes, this piece originally formed part of
a sash. The regularly spaced motifs have
been chosen to complement both the cloth
and its application.

**Silk, France, 1736–39**

A woven panel with a pattern of shells and
flowers mixes the most costly of materials
with the most complex of weaving
techniques: brocading. This particular
design uses polychrome and real silver
threads to create the pattern.

**Silk, detail, England, 1740–45**

The shell, the most important rococo motif,
forms the basis of the pattern on this grand
embroidered mantua or court dress, and is
combined with an abundance of realistic
flowers. The botanically correct depiction of
flowers was a feature of rococo embroidery.

**Lace, detail, Flanders, mid 18th century**
A characteristic of Mechlin lace, like this, was the use of a distinctive, shiny thread to outline its motifs. This gave it a clarity that made it suitable for pictorial designs like this basket of fruit, which features on the crown of this cap of bobbin lace.

**Cotton, France, late 18th century**
A printed panel that deftly combines two strong influences of its period: naturalism and neoclassicism. A lavishly filled and garlanded floral basket alternates with pictorial medallions featuring an agricultural worker.

**Cotton, Ottoman Empire, 19th century**
This napkin is embroidered with silk and metal thread. This rigid and heavily stylised patterning on the border shows a repeated branch with leaves, interspersed with a floral basket or container, both rather naive in appearance.

**Cotton, Ottoman Empire, mid 19th century**
Embroidered textiles were an essential part of daily life in the Ottoman world. They were used to wrap gifts, to decorate rooms, as linen and as clothing. This cotton towel, densely embroidered with silk and metal thread, has stylised plants set in a border.

# Bouquets

### 18th–20th Century

Bouquets have been used for gifts and at ceremonial occasions for centuries. In textile patterning they are part of the wider use of natural imagery. The selection here features principally roses and other English flowers in a variety of groupings. Bouquet patterns especially suit the 'island' style of stand-alone motifs arranged either in columns or in drop repeats. Symbolically, bouquets can be used to represent spiritual perfection, in reference to the gift of the 'mystic rose' to Mary from St John of the Cross.

**Linen, detail, England, c.1780–1810**
This block-print pattern featuring islands of bunches of flowers, each tied with a ribbon bow, offers a fine, naturalistic rendering of a number of flowers, among them the cabbage rose, auricula, lilac and morning glory.

**Cotton, England, 1830s**
A lavish design of roses, columbines, hollyhocks and peonies is used as a vertical repeat on this glazed and printed fabric. A vertical stripe divides the sections of the pattern. The small butterfly, perched on the right, complements the naturalistic rendering.

### Cotton, England, 1830s

Naturalistically rendered branches of roses and leaves climb in a vertical pattern up this printed, glazed fabric. Patterns such as this are particularly good for use as curtains or hangings.

### Cotton, England, 1840s

The Victorians loved natural images, and in their language of flowers, widely understood at the time, this design sends a mixed message of 'pride' from the rose and 'heaven' from the delphinium. Large, florid bouquets printed onto a plain ground are characteristic of this period, as is the shiny, glazed finish on this printed chintz.

### Silk, France, 1937

A stylish crêpe dress fabric designed by François Ducharne is printed with a vertical repeat of lily flowers and stems. The high contrast between the white and yellow flowers and the black background means that the pattern appears to float on the material.

# Floral On Patterned Ground

### 17th–18th century

These examples, from a wide range of sources, show how pattern can be overlaid in layers, or used as contrast with one another within the same piece. This double patterning device allows greater scope for the designer and offers more complex images for the user to enjoy. The effect can be achieved in various ways, from a simple juxtaposition of contrasting elements such as flowers and lines, to complex arrangements that build up the design bit by bit. In many cases there is a fundamental framework, such as squares, ogees or panels, that forms the basis of the pattern.

**Silk, fragment, Japan, 17th century**

A luxurious design treatment, (left) in which the ground fabric is decorated with applied gold leaf, tie-dyeing (*shibori*) and embroidery, sets off motifs of cascading flowers and circular and staggered diamonds motifs, on a basketwork background.

**Design for a silk, England, c.1718**

A pencil and watercolour treatment adornes this woven fabric by Christopher Baudouin. Vertical stripes of pale green with pink edges separate wider panels with three different types of orange flowers and pale-green leaves; and the design is punctuated by a neat yellow dot between the main motifs.

**Carpet, detail, India, 19th century**
Hand-knotted in wool on a silk and cotton weft, the diamond lattice of this piece has been used as a useful patterning tool to make frames. Each diamond in this design is filled with a different species of flower, and is mirrored by the diamond that is placed immediately below or to the side of it.

**Silk, England, c.1880**
Designed by the artist George Charles Haite, the tiled grid pattern of this fabric is overlaid by a plethora of motifs, including ornate sunflowers, birds, bats, the sun and moon. The sunflower was particularly favoured by the followers of the Aesthetic Movement and appeared on everything from tiles to teapots.

**Cotton, England, c.1921**
This diagonal repeating pattern is a furnishing fabric with a particularly bold and rich design: the background trellis is overlaid with large clusters of pink, purple and amber flowers and bunches of grapes.

# Garlands & Ribbons

### 17th–18th Century

This group of patterns uses flowers in a stylised manner, often relying on meandering stems and garlands to create the repeating framework of the design. Their intrinsic colours and shapes make them immediately appealing to the eye and they remained popular in various forms from the 17th century onwards. The obvious attractiveness of these patterns lies in the apparently informal arrangements, which often look as if they have been scattered or randomly placed. When seen in larger pieces, however, the formal repeat is usually evident.

**Linen and cotton, England, mid 17th century**

Embroidered in the technique known as crewel-work – from the crewel or worsted wool used to work the pattern – this curtain features a design with an offset horizontal repeat. The flowers and leaves are apparently linked by a continuous spiral stem.

### Silk, detail, France, c.1700

A delightful painted hanging with a diaper framework of climbing plants, showcases motifs including flower pots, bamboo and small pagoda-style houses: a clear reference to the popularity of imported Chinese patterns.

### Cotton, detail, India, 18th century

The graceful and sinuous climbing plant on a block-printed dress fabric has smaller island-type patterns of a different flower inserted into the spaces created by the flexing tendrils.

### Cotton, England, c.1700–25

Inspiration for patterns such as this delicate and dainty rendering of flowers and stems on this embroidered curtain came from engravings and from other images that were published for use by needlewomen.

### Design for silk, England, c.1752

A pencil and watercolour design for damask by Anna Maria Garthwaite, who was born in 1690 and became a leading pattern designer in the English silk industry. The drawing shows a flowered pattern in the rococo style, with a characteristic emphasis on asymmetrical structures and winding curves.

# FLORA Chintz

### Indian, 18th Century

The chintzes produced in India were different from those made later in Europe. The Indians were among the first to develop the skills of painting on cotton cloth using mordants and dyes. These painted and printed cloths were highly sought-after in Europe in the 17th and 18th centuries. The name chintz comes from *chitta*, meaning spotted or speckled. The designs were initially based on Indian artists' close observation of flora and fauna, but the designs gradually changed to suit Western tastes (*see pages 74–5*). Chintzes were used for curtains, bed and wall hangings and clothing.

**Cotton, India, 18th century**
A typical example of a chintz floral pattern with red flowers on a red-spotted ground. The meticulously drawn and very attractively produced design is one example amongst many that demonstrate the inventiveness of Indian designers in creating patterns directly for the European market.

**Cotton, India, c.1715–25**

This length of chintz was probably used as dress material as it is very fine. It is unusual in that the French-woven 'bizarre' silks that were fashionable at the time have influenced its design. They had strong, linear patterns, and often included exotic-looking objects.

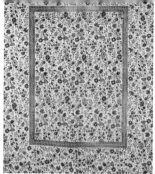

**Cotton, India, c.1725–50**

A quilted chintz bed cover, made for the Western market in south-east India and featuring a small floral design perhaps more associated with dress material than bed furnishings. The field and the frame are separated by a delicate border with a pointed motif.

**Cotton, detail, India, mid 18th century**

A bucolic Indian rendition of a hunting scene, surrounded by a floral swag, this patterned cotton has clearly been produced for the European market. It nevertheless retains a rather exotic air. The delicately painted piece of chintz was intended for use as a petticoat.

**Cotton, detail, India, c.1770s**

Painted and dyed, this cotton valance forms part of some famous bed furnishings presented to Mrs David Garrick in 1775 by friends in Calcutta. These hangings, once impounded by Customs, were made in Masulipatam, Madras, in an East India Company factory.

# FLORA Chintz

### English, 19th Century

The ubiquity of chintz, especially as a furnishing fabric for the English country house or cottage, is well known, and the word has passed into common usage for any printed floral cotton. The European production of chintz developed from the original imports from India (*see pages 72–3*). During the 19th century chintz manufacturers developed enormous ranges of prints with great variety and originality of patterning. Both France and England excelled at producing patterns, the French designs being more formal and the English often using flowers in a variety of groupings.

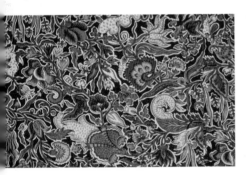

**Cotton, England, c.1805–10**
Very similar to a French design, this English fabric may be a copy, or both may have taken their inspiration from the same Indian source. Bannister Hall, in Preston, was the leading manufacturer of this sort of textile, a polychrome block-printed with blue pencilling.

**Cotton, England, c.1825**
A good example of the possibilities of changing patterns simply by altering the background shade, this block-printed cotton resist is set on a dipped blue ground. It features semi-stylised flowers and leaves, bordered by a chain pattern in columns.

**Cotton, England, 1827**

Lightly printed fern-like leaves were popular from 1826 until 1830. This block-printed chintz has been given a glazed surface, which was achieved by putting it through various finishing processes. The sheen was lost in washing, but reglazing was possible.

**Cotton, England, 1836**

A complex design featuring four distinct elements in the pattern. The floral bouquets are linked together with a representation of a cloth scarf, surrounded by gilded stylised stems, all of which are imposed on a small fretted, diaper-type background.

**Cotton, England, c.1850**

This printed chintz, called 'Hollyhock', has a naturalistic floral design that, although popular, was condemned by design reformers. It was exhibited in 1852 in an exhibition called 'False Principles in Design', where it was damned for its 'Direct Imitation of Nature'.

# Naturalistic

### 20th Century

Flowers offer the designer almost unlimited freedom, with the sheer variety of shapes, colours and possible arrangements giving unending inspiration. They can be botanically close copies of particular flowers; they can be semi-stylised so that the flower is recognisable but is reconfigured slightly; or they can be completely abstracted. Although individual flowers have their own specific symbolism, flowers in general are symbols of the passive state, of harmony and innocence, and are most frequently used purely for decorative effect.

**Cotton, England, c.1891**
Designed by John Henry Dearle and block-printed by Morris & Co., this floral, repeating pattern is called 'Daffodil'. It reflects Dearle's later work, which was influenced by the complexity and weaving lines of Near Eastern patterns. However, in the Victorian language of flowers, the daffodil represents regard for someone.

**Linen, England, 1930**
A pattern by Arthur Sanderson & Sons, featuring all-over flowers of types typical of an English country garden. The Victorians, heavily aware of symbolism, might have chosen delphinium and phlox for their meanings (fickleness and unanimity, respectively) but they were probably chosen for their harmonious colours.

**Cotton, England, 1932**
Colourful crocuses set on a blue background seem full of optimism in a cheerful design produced by Arthur Sanderson & Sons. The crocus symbolises youthful gladness and is widely seen as an indication of the renewal coming with springtime.

**Silk, England, 2008**
A modern take on a traditional floral image of morning glory that usually represents affection. This design by Clarissa Hulse has a wonderful ethereal quality, in part created by the soft shadows of the image and the long line of the delicately falling tendrils.

**Linen, England, 2008**
In this abstracted floral design by Neisha Crossland, the weaving stems create a pattern of roundels similar to early 17th-century embroidery. The colour scheme of tangerine on a bisque stone background, though, is thoroughly of the 21st century.

# Victorian Symbolism

### 19th–20th Century

For the Victorians, the language of flowers was very popular, although the symbolic use of flowers dates back to antiquity. In medieval and Renaissance culture, flowers were often given moral meanings. This is most apparent in art, in which the saints are depicted with flowers that are symbolic of their virtues. Although we cannot be certain whether patterns of a particular plant were intended to offer a symbolic interpretation, the popular imagination will often make connections of its own.

**Wool and cotton, England, c.1851**
A woven damask featuring the Gothic motifs particularly associated with A.W.N Pugin – an architect and designer who pioneered the revival of neo-Gothic design. Pugin laid the foundations for an aesthetic that favoured stylised designs over naturalistic ones.

**Cotton, England, 1873**

Highly characteristic of the work of Morris & Co., this pattern uses a mix of tulips and willows, and was designed by William Morris himself. The tulip symbolises fame while the willow is associated with loss, grief and death.

**Silk, England, 1876**

The honeysuckle symbolises generous and devoted affection and/or sweetness of disposition. In this pattern, the designer William Morris has used his knowledge of plants to create one of the sophisticated yet relaxing patterns that were to become a hallmark of his work.

**Cotton, England, 1888**

A typical late 19th-century pattern for a printed furnishing fabric. The large ornate leaves and floral scroll decoration are brought together by Lewis Foreman Day, one of the most successful designers of the period. Interpreted in the language of flowers, the pinks convey love, but the willow refers to lost love.

**Paper, England, early 20th century**

This design, by the Silver Studios, for fabric is entitled 'Green Hemlock', a plant traditionally associated with death and the supernatural. However, it is unlikely that the makers intended too dark an interpretation: vaguely 'mystical' links appealed to the sensibilities of the Art Nouveau period.

# FLORA Stylised

## 20th Century

In the early 20th century, the early stylisation of forms was associated with the Art Nouveau and Art Deco approaches to design. In many cases the origin of the flower that has been transformed is still evident, but in others its identity has been lost in the process. These designs, combined with the novel colours made possible by developments in chemical dyeing, created some very vibrant and exciting textiles. The symbolism may have lessened but the value of flowers in pattern remains undiminished.

**Design for textile, Scotland, 19th–20th century**
A characteristic work by Charles Rennie Mackintosh features his ubiquitous and very recognisable rose form paired with a loose geometric framework made up of plain and beaded lines. The rose is a symbol of perfection and love.

**Cotton and linen, England, 1903**

The crocus is a symbol of cheerfulness and love of justice. In this design for a furnishing fabric by George Haite, the crocus has been stylised into scrolling swirls that repeat across the pattern. The petals are outlined in heavy, darker lines.

**Cotton, England, 1906**

A regular pattern of stylised tulips standing straight, with a large leaf behind the flower heads and smaller, slightly curled leaves to the side, is slightly typical of the Art Nouveau style. The red tulip symbolises everlasting love.

**Page from a textile sample book, Japan, 1938**

A design for a textile entitled 'Poppies'. The simple design of white flowers with green and grey leaves on a pink ground has a slightly wistful quality, appropriate to a flower which is a symbol for dreams.

**Cotton, China, c.1978**

The vertical emphasis of this printed pattern defines its use as a bed covering. It features large peony flowers, which represent riches and honour, and peacocks, which represent beauty and dignity, as well as the Temple of Heaven in Beijing.

# Introduction

Second only to flowers, animals, birds and insects are the most popular themes for pattern-makers. Whether in realistic or mythological, abstract or stylised representations, fauna are part of the staple diet of the designer. Specific ideas or symbolism are associated with certain species: among them cranes, peacocks, horses and elephants, in particular, come with many potent beliefs and superstitions in different cultures. In addition to looking at the depiction of particular animals, this section includes some of the many patterns based on insect and marine life.

**Linen, detail, England, early 17th century**
A charming and naïve depiction of wildlife on this embroidered cover includes a running rabbit ornamented with gold and silver spots in blue squares, a small bird, and a caterpillar, outlined in red. Each of these subjects has its own symbolism, but in this piece it seems that the designer's intention was simply to show the fauna of the countryside ornamentally.

**Wool, detail, Netherlands, mid 18th century**

A close-up view of an ostrich, which is just one of a number of exotic subjects featuring on a petticoat, handknitted in beige, and rendered in purl stitches against a stocking-stitch ground. The ostrich is a symbol of faith and contemplation.

**Silk, fragment, Japan, 19th century**

Found mounted in an album, this gauze-weave textile has resist-dyed decoration (*yuzen*). The pattern depicts a squirrel on a vine. The squirrel (a symbol of trust and thrift) represents fertility in Japan.

**Cotton, England, 1882**

The indigo-discharged and block-printed furnishing fabric entitled 'Brother Rabbit' (right) is designed by William Morris. A formal repeating pattern is typical of his work and was apparently inspired by the *Uncle Remus* stories that Morris read to his young family.

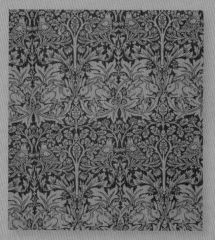

**Tapestry, detail, England, 1887**

William Morris and Philip Webb designed 'The Forest' as shown here below. The pattern places five studies of animals and birds within a thick cover of trailing acanthus leaves, one of Morris's favoured classical motifs. This detail shows the lion.

# Insects

### 17th–21st Century

Although bugs might not at first seem ideal subjects for pattern-making, they feature frequently. Beetles or bees, crickets or cicadas, insects offer rich imagery, are decorative in their own right, and have symbolic meanings. The bee, for example, is a symbol of the imposing of civilisation and order by means of wisdom and force and was widely used during the imperial reign of Napoleon I. With their small scale and elaborate structure, insects were also a common choice to show off virtuoso sewing skills in an age when fine needlework was an important social accomplishment.

**Velvet, detail, England, c.1600**
Extraordinarily elaborate, this pile silk cushion cover is ornamented with applied shapes of linen canvas, densely embroidered with silk and metal threads in tent stitch, laid and couched work. Worms, caterpillars and craneflies are depicted, on the same scale as animals such as dogs and elephants. The effect is naïve, but charming.

### Satin, England, c.1600

A rather bizarre composition is embroidered on this panel, originally for a petticoat. Jagged arrows, an obelisk and an armillary sphere vie for space with a spider's web – the latter without its occupant. Odd though the subject matter is, it is richly applied with coloured silks and gilt thread.

### Linen, detail, England, c.1609–29

The overall design of the cover from which this piece is drawn features scrolls, animals, birds and flowers. This little corner shows a part of one of the flowers and a caterpillar, clearly rendered in silk silver and silver-gilt thread, though not naturalistic.

### Lace, detail, France, early 1800s

The bee played an important part in the symbolism of France during the First Empire (1804–14) representing the strong ruler of an ordered empire. This triangular lace scarf or *fichu* was worn to indicate its owner's loyalty to the Emperor.

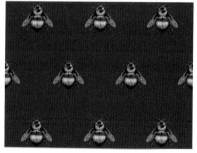

### Velvet, Scotland, 2008

This modern take on the Napoleonic motif designed by Timorous Beasties, a company founded in Glasgow in 1990, demonstrates how a simple change in scale can affect the impact of a pattern. The bee is here produced outsize, which has the effect of turning it into a strong statement that you either love or hate.

# Butterflies

### 18th–20th Century

The colour and delicacy of butterflies has proved inspirational for many designers and pattern-makers. The life cycle of the butterfly, with its metamorphosis from larva to winged beauty has a symbolic value, too, and plays a part in many myths and stories – in the story of Psyche, for example, the beautiful young woman is often depicted with butterfly wings as a symbol of resurrection. The butterfly is also, unsurprisingly, often associated with patterns intended for women because of the grace they both share.

**Cotton, detail, India, c.1720–40**
A painted and dyed chintz *palampore* from the Coromandel Coast shows how scattered small motifs, in this case butterflies and birds, can be used to fill empty spaces in the border. The main design of the piece features small insects, birds and crabs and the overall pattern has some similarities to contemporary ceramic designs.

**Lace, England, 1878**
A fan leaf of worked bobbin lace by Emma Radford demonstrates the naturalism in design associated with lace produced at Honiton, Devon. Flowers, fruit, leaves and insects are all clearly taken from nature and are easily recognisable even in the all-white form.

**Silk, Japan, 1884**

A delightful pattern of thistle and butterfly features in this silk-embroidered textile found in a sample book and originating in Kyoto. In Japan, the grace and airy lightness of the butterfly has associations with women and femininity. Two butterflies shown together indicate marital happiness.

**Cotton, England, c.1920**

Designed by Minnie McLeish this roller-printed furnishing fabric was shown at the Paris Exposition des Arts Décoratifs in 1925. The abstraction of the flower and insect form is typical of Art Deco patterns, but also makes clear reference to the printed silk designs of the early 18th-century.

**Silk, Austria, c.1925**

Produced by the guild of designers/ makers called the Wiener Werkstätte (Vienna Workshop), this printed dress fabric displays the basic forms and bright colours that characterised their textiles. The patterns were derived from Eastern European peasant art and geometric motifs.

# Marine Life

### 19th–20th Century

The use of imagery from the sea for textile patterning can be traced back as far as early Egyptian work, in which swimming fish are depicted on cloth. Although the Christian iconography of the fish and the fisherman is well known, fish also have symbolic meanings in other cultures. In China they are a symbol of good luck and, elsewhere can also represent water, life and fertility. In Japanese culture, the koi carp represents strength of purpose and perseverance in harsh conditions.

**Cotton, detail, Japan, 19th century**

A futon cover, or *futon-ji*, with paste-resist decoration (*tsutsugaki*), depicting fish contained in roundels and surrounded by other round geometric shapes, including a stylised crane as a symbol of longevity. This combination of bird and fish is perceived as auspicious.

**Bast fibre, detail, Japan, 19th century**
This length of paste-resist dyed decoration cloth was originally created for use as kimono fabric. It is woven from hemp fibres. The design, of fish by riverside flowers, suggests the calming and relaxed pleasures of sitting on a river bank.

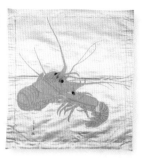

**Silk, Japan, 19th century**
This satin *fukusa*, or sewn cover for a gift, has embroidery depicting two lobsters that represent Izanami-no-mikoto, the goddess of creation, and Izanagi-no-mikoto, her husband. This primordial couple is enshrined at Ise, the most important Shinto shrine in Japan.

**Cotton, detail, Japan, early 20th century**
*Noren*, or doorway curtains, are made from panels of cloth sewn together at the top. They are used at the doors of retail shops and their designs function as advertisements. This *noren*, with its arresting octopus motif, may well have covered the door of a business specialising in seafood.

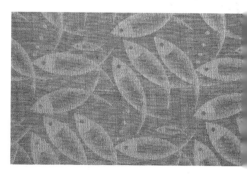

**Linen, Ireland, c.1935**
An elegant reversible linen, entitled 'Mandalay', depicts a stylised shoal of fish swimming in pairs and threes. This is a particularly refined example of an Art Deco design, with a typical feel of movement inherent in it.

# Birds

### Ancient and Modern

Examples of textiles depicting birds exist from early Egyptian times, and as a decorative motif birds have sustained their popularity ever since. Whether stylised or naturalistic, most species have been used in pattern design at one time or another, from small dainty songbirds to peacocks, cranes and eagles. Their ability to fly is often used to symbolise the links between heaven and earth, and has also been used to represent spiritual states, angels and higher forms of being. However, it is uncommon to see black or dark birds used in textile designs, as in many countries they symbolise bad luck or even death.

**Tapestry, detail, Egypt, 4th–5th century**
An early woven linen panel depicting a quail worked in purple wool with red, pink and yellow details. The quail, a symbol of the cycle of life, is a common motif on early Egyptian decorative panels.

**Tapestry, detail, England, 19th century**
William Morris used pairs of birds in a number of his popular patterns from the late 1870s onwards. Here, the accurate depiction shows Morris's familiarity with British birds, which he closely observed in his country garden.

**Cotton, Japan, 19th century**
A traditional resist-dyed or *bingata* cloth, from Ryukyu Islands, features stylised birds and flowers in dark blue and white, and was made using stencils and freehand painting. *Bingata* are generally bright-coloured and may include assorted patterns, usually depicting natural subjects.

**Cotton, England, 1830s**
The repeated pattern of birds and a trailing floral spray, very naturalistically rendered, is the key feature of this roller-printed furnishing fabric. The design is taken from a printing plate from *The Birds of America* by John James Audubon and is part of a series produced using his designs.

### Cotton, England, 1830s

The design here, by J.J. Audubon, depicting birds, flowers and pine cones, reflects the strong interest felt at this period in the natural world. It is rendered on a roller-printed furnishing fabric; extra colours would have been added to the design with a surface roller.

### Silk, detail, Japan, mid 19th century

Detail of a kimono with a design called 'Ducks on Rippling Water with Flowers'. This satin kimono has silk embroidery showing a deep-blue river landscape with water reeds, flowers and Mandarin ducks on rippling water, which symbolise marital harmony.

### Velvet, England, c. 1850–74

Used for the bodice of a woman's dress, this black fabric is heavily embroidered with blue and cream birds and butterflies. Clothing was often very elaborately trimmed and ornamented in the mid 19th century, and motifs drawn from the natural world were popular.

**Cotton, England, 1883**
'Strawberry Thief' is one of the best known furnishing fabrics by William Morris, with birds by Philip Webb. The print, featuring long-tailed and short-tailed thrushes amid green foliage, blue acanthus leaves and red strawberries against a dark blue background is a typical Arts and Crafts design.

**(Unknown), Britain, 1930s**
This printed furnishing fabric entitled 'Swans' was designed by Eileen Hunter. The stylised white motifs are recognisably swan-like. The effect is heightened by the contrast between the light and dark areas, confusing the eye into making different sets of shapes from what it sees.

**Silk, detail, England, 1966**
A screenprinted fabric by the Ascher Studio, London. Its design of swallows, branches and blossom is influenced by Japanese motifs, as is the lilac background. The 1960s saw a revival of interest in Japanese imagery, which was seen as simultaneously traditional and modern.

# Cranes & Geese

### 17th–20th Century

Although much associated with China and especially Japan, cranes and geese also appear in textiles from other cultures. In Taoism the crane is a symbol of immortality and in Japan it represents longevity. Its white feathers stand for purity, while its red head is believed to show the stamina of its life force. Its annual return from migration was seen as a symbol of regeneration and it is often shown with plum blossom as a sign of spring. In some cultures, the goose is represented as an intermediary between heaven and earth.

**Silk, Korea, c.1600–1700**

Korean iconography on rank badges such as this is distinct, featuring single or paired birds and animals set in stylised rocks amongst waves. The piece is decorated in silk threads and shows a single crane holding the plant of eternal youth in a formalised landscape.

**Satin, China, 18th–19th century**

The pattern on this 'Mandarin square' or rank badge shows a wild goose, symbolically a carrier of good omens, flying against a tightly scrolled background. It signifies that its bearer is of the 4th rank and would have been worn on a surcoat. The pattern is densely embroidered in silk and gold threads.

**Silk, detail, Japan, 19th century**

A *fukusa* is an elaborately decorated square of cloth used to cover a gift during its formal presentation. This satin silk example has embroidered flying golden cranes with red caps, on a deep-blue ground. The asymmetry of the pattern makes it visually stimulating.

**Silk, Japan, 19th century**

A woven satin *fukusa*, or gift cover, depicts flying golden cranes with black feathers and red caps, made in silk embroidery on a deep-blue ground. Elaborately decorated covers were a key part of the ceremony of gift giving and reflected the status and taste of the donor.

**Cotton, Britain, 1948**

The central vertical lozenge pattern is reflected by zigzag lines on the background, and balanced by repeated images of small birds and other wildlife. A wax-resist print design by the Manchester-based firm Logan, Muckett and Co. for the export market to West Africa.

# Peacocks

### 18th–20th Century

Widely familiar in the West as an image of vanity, historically the peacock has held more importance as a symbol of the sun. In classical mythology it was sacred to Zeus's wife Hera, but it has had a range of emblematic and symbolic roles in other cultures too. In Burma it was the emblem of the monarchy; in India it is perceived as a destroyer of serpents and has links to immortality; while to Muslims the peacock is a cosmic symbol. Peacock imagery was popular in European patterns in the late 19th century and was associated with the Aesthetic Movement, which developed a cult of beauty in art and design and used it decoratively.

**Cotton, England, 1761**
'Old Ford', a copperplate print by Robert Jones & Co., shows a pastoral scene with an exotic peacock strutting amongst classical ruins. This sort of dense pictorial pattern was popular in the mid 18th century.

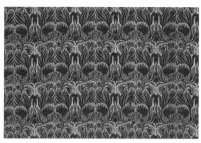

**Wool, England, 1878**
'Peacock and Dragon', a design by William Morris, is one in which he was intentionally drawing on traditional Islamic colours and motifs. The paired confronting peacocks, sitting on either side of the Tree of Life, reference the Eastern idea of the twofold nature of the human psyche.

**Cotton, England, c.1882**
The peacock motif, in conjunction with the stylised foliage, is given a very formal and symmetrical repeat in this printed fabric by A.H. MacMurdo of the Century Guild. Guild members designed decorative artworks, including textiles, that were then manufactured for them.

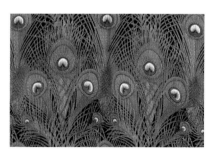

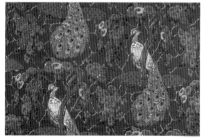

**Cotton, England, c.1887**
This well-known design, 'Peacock Feathers', which has long been associated with Liberty and Co., was designed by Arthur Silver of the Silver Studios. As a representation of one's own beauty, the peacock feather had particular resonance for members of the Aesthetic Movement.

**Cotton, England, c.1922**
An exotically patterned roller-printed fabric intended for furnishing. It has a regular, repeating pattern featuring purple, brown and white peacock motifs perched on branches of pink blossom.

# Horses

### 16th–20th Century

Whether the horse represents the creature of darkness and magical powers, a bringer of death, a water god, a driving force, a creature of the sun or the steed of the gods, it exercises a powerful pull on our collective psyches and it has been a symbol of power in many cultures from very early times. In pattern, horses are shown in all moods: in some tamed and depicted in rural surroundings, while in others horses are more associated with speed and independent power.

**Tapestry, England, c. 1590–1620**
A woven valance for a bed, made at the Sheldon workshops. The idealised hunting scene, complete with prancing horse, hounds and huntsmen on foot, is separated by vases of fruit and flowers from other pursuits in the pattern. A naïve sense of depth is given by the receding hills in the background.

**Cotton, India, mid 18th century**

A southern Indian product made for the European market, this piece for a petticoat includes Western figures and horse riders in its border design. At this date the garment was intended to be worn under an open dress, and to be seen.

**Cotton, France, c.1840**

This toile-like print from Alsace shows vignettes of rural life, with the tame horse as a servant of humans. Small framed images such as these were typical of the 1840s, when pastoral themes, often scenes taken from popular literature, were repeated amongst a foliate framework.

**Cotton, Pakistan, c.1880**

Produced in Kamalia, in the Punjab, this printed wall hanging has a highly regimented pattern, with up to ten bands of different pictures and motifs making up the complete design. The prancing horses feature in a formal parade and act as a good foil to the rigid flowers in the middle.

**Cotton, England, 1948**

'Horse Heads', a print designed by John Drummond, is an energetic depiction of all the muscle and strength associated with the horse. A simple half-drop repeat, with scattered and abstract shapes used as infill, is characteristic of this period. Another interpretation might see this as a sea horse.

# Elephants

### 16th–19th Century

Symbols of wealth, prosperity and stability, elephants hold a special place in Asian culture. Indra, lord of the heavens in Hindu mythology, is usually shown riding an elephant, symbolising the power of kingship. In Southeast Asia, a white elephant is believed to grant rainfall and a good harvest. In Buddhism, an elephant shown on its own signifies the Buddha's conception, whilst set on a column it evokes enlightenment. Finally, the elephant can be identified in Asian symbolism with support of the cosmos: four pillars (the legs) holding a sphere (its body).

**Silk, fragment, India, 16th century**
This fragment of a textile or hanging features a woven pattern that depicts an elephant and rider, the latter in the process of releasing an arrow. The oddity of scale does not detract from the overall effect of this delightful textile, which is now rather faded.

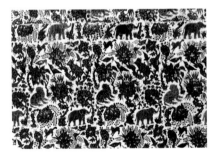

**Cotton, detail, India, c.1640–80**
A chintz bedspread from the Coromandel Coast featuring a repeating pattern of elephants amongst other animals and flora. This bright, unconstrained and cheerful design is typical of the products of the period and the location.

## Textile sample, detail, India, 19th century

A domestic embroidery, created in dense chain stitch, typical of the work from Kutch, in north-west Gujarat. It depicts a blue elephant in a walking pose, complete with howdah, saddle cloth and a feathered plume. There are flower motifs on either side and the colourful composition is set off by a deep pink ground.

## Silk, detail, India, 1855

A woven silk sari pattern from Bengal depicting men sitting on chairs reading, whilst a parade of decorated elephants, with attendants with flags, passes by. A border of diapers and a traditional *boteh* or paisley pattern frames the scene.

## Cotton, detail, India, c.1897

A coverlet or *kantha*, quilted and embroidered with white and coloured cotton, mainly in running stitch, and ornamented with naïve designs, including a pair of charmingly primitive elephants. Covers such as these were often made from worn-out saris.

# Mythological

### 17th–19th Century

Wherever there is a tradition of myth-making or even story-telling, the mythological themes and images will be transferred to textiles. It is always a moot point whether a particular example is actually intended to reflect the mythology apparently depicted or whether it is being used in a decorative rather than a symbolic way. In cases where patterns have been appropriated from other cultures such second-hand use is common. An accurate reading of a pattern will always depend a great deal upon the context of the original pattern and its intended use.

**Linen and cotton, England, late 17th century**
A textile used as a bed hanging, embroidered in crewel wool with fantastical creatures and plants. These hangings feature trees derived from Indian painted textiles and a range of animals, some with a heraldic look, taken from traditional English sources.

**Linen, detail, Greece, 18th century**
A fantastical multi-coloured cock/hen is embroidered at one end of this cushion cover from Skyros. The cockerel is a universal solar symbol, although in Greek legend it is the specific attribute of Apollo, the bringer of the dawn.

**Satin, China, 18th–19th century**

A silk-embroidered Mandarin insignia
(a badge for a judge) featuring the ancient
Chinese supernatural animal, the *Hsieh-
Chai*. Goat-like in appearance, but with
only one horn, it is endowed with the
appropriate faculty of detecting the guilty.

**Silk, detail, Japan, late 19th century**

Part of a kimono embroidered with silk
and metallic threads, showing a dragon
amongst simple curled cloud shapes.
Both the motif and its rendering are
typically Japanese. Most Japanese dragons
are water deities, and the clouds also
reference this attribute.

**Wool and silk, detail, England, 1887**

William Morris was one of several designers
responsible for this tapestry, woven on a
cotton warp. It depicts animals and birds
sitting in a forest, undisturbed by humans.
This detail shows a peacock against a
scrolled acanthus leaf.

# Introduction

The term 'stylised' refers to a set of artistic forms and conventions that are used by pattern-makers to create particular and recognised effects. These effects are not natural or spontaneous, but represent a conventionalised idea of an image or adaptation of a shape. They are particularly important in pattern-making for textiles because they often enable a design to be planned with formal or regular repeats. Examples of stylisation are myriad, but some principal forms, such as arabesques, scrolls, ogees, roundels and *botehs* (paisley), are widely used around the world. The stylised patterns in this section demonstrate the range of possibilities.

**Cotton, India, c.1510**
A block-printed textile for ceremonial use from Gujarat that features the *hamsa* or stylised goose design. Originally the goose signified strength and virility. Later, the *hamsa* acquired more symbolic attributes, including purity, detachment, divine knowledge, cosmic breath (*prana*) and the highest spiritual achievement.

### Velvet, Turkey, 16th century

The dominant motif shown is a stylised, fan-like carnation and is one of the most typical Ottoman textile patterns. This version, taken from a silk furnishing fabric and incorporating metal threads, is particularly luxurious.

### Silk, Italy, 17th century

This luxurious example of stylisation on a furnishing fabric features a highly organised mixture of flowers and animal shapes within a formal scrolled framework. The animal faces inwards along the body of the scroll, and outwards where the scroll parts open.

### Silk, England, 1850–70

A stylised arabesque pattern based on the intricate inter-weaving of flowing lines features on this woven fabric, intended for furnishings. The arabesque, which is classical in origin, was revived during the Renaissance. It was also influenced by Near Eastern pattern-making, especially the ogee shape.

### Silk and wool, England, 1870

One of the earliest commercial designs of Christopher Dresser, this Jacquard-woven curtain demonstrates how earlier forms can influence later work. The traditional geometric framework of A.W.N. Pugin surrounds the stylised floral patterns, which are derived from Eastern sources.

# Ogee

### 16th–20th Century

An ogee is defined as a shape made by two unbroken confronting concave and convex curves. It is based on the S shape and is often associated with decorative mouldings, having been introduced to Europe as a form for architectural features such as windows and arches from the Middle East. It was soon transferred to textiles, where it could be stretched vertically – to make a shape resembling a glass Christmas decoration – or horizontally. The ogee often forms the basis of a naturalistic or abstract pattern.

**Silk, Turkey, 16th century**
The design of this woven brocade is based on staggered rows of pointed-oval medallions. Each has a gold tulip plant at its centre. The spaces between the medallions are filled with two intertwining vines. One is set with pomegranates, the other with tulip flowers.

**Velvet, Turkey, 16th century**
This Ottoman silk furnishing fabric embellished with metal threads is a direct imitation of an Italian design. The ogival trellis motif, with its regular and symmetrical pattern system, is typical of Italian work of the period.

**Silk and cotton, Turkey, 16th–17th century**
A hand-woven kaftan featuring silver-gilt thread and decorated with floral designs over a basic ogee-shaped outline. Garments like this were preserved in imperial tombs, where they were laid over the graves of the deceased.

**Velvet, Turkey, 17th century**
A regular pattern, though with subtle variations, of large eight-lobed floral motifs, ornamented with flowers and leaves, in old gold on a deep-red silk ground. The pattern is based on staggered rows of medallions framed by vines set with flowers.

**Cotton and rayon, England, 1925**
Entitled 'Whitchurch', this fabric was woven to incorporate bright design highlights through the use of metallic and vivid rayon thread. The debt it owes to Renaissance Italian designs is evident in the application of the ogee shapes.

# Formal

### 19th Century

Formal geometry is the base for many textile patterns. Whether as a result of the fabric's construction (for example, a woven stripe) or of applied decoration, such as a geometric print. The selection here shows ogees, circles and diamond shapes that have been manipulated to create regular repeats. The use of shapes like these reflects an interest in medieval compass work, which would have exerted an influence over mid to late 19th-century designers.

**Cotton, England, c.1845–51**
This is a rare design for a glazed block-print to be used as a curtain or blind, by A.W.N. Pugin. The Gothic arabesque design reflects his interest in medieval patterns. It was registered at the Public Record Office as no. 69572, on 28 May 1850.

**Silk, England, c.1874**

The pattern here is loosely derived from two sources: medieval decoration and Japanese designs. It was designed by E.W. Godwin, a pioneer in the Anglo-Japanese style fashionable in the 1870s, and is entitled 'Syringa'.

**Silk, England, c.1874–6**

The design for this Jacquard weave, again the work of E.W. Godwin, is a typical example of the fashionable Anglo-Japanese style of the later 19th century. The central feature, magnolia blossom, representing a love of nature, comes directly from a Japanese crest.

**Velvet, England, 1884**

Designed by William Morris, this woven-silk brocade is named 'Granada'. The pattern is based on two series of stems that create overlapping ogee shapes. Pomegranates, the classic fertility symbol, and a favoured motif for Arts and Crafts designers in the late 19th century, are placed at the intersections.

**Cotton, England, 1888**

The source of the pattern for this block-printed velveteen designed by Lewis Foreman Day is to be found in the tiles made at the Iznik potteries in Turkey, which were highly sought-after for interiors during the 1880s.

# Small Repeats

### 18th–20th Century

Repeating patterns are the lifeblood of much textile design, but there are particular sets of stylised imagery that lend themselves specifically to small or large repeats. This group of small repeats demonstrates how a pattern can be delicate and unassertive, acting as a good background for other furnishings. Often comprising isolated shapes over the whole fabric, small repeats may be either regimented or apparently random. However, the use of stylised floral forms, foliage and geometric shapes are particularly characteristic of this approach to patterning.

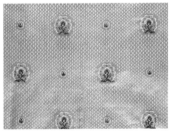

**Cotton, India, 1772**
Systematically organised, offset rows of floral motifs have their origins in Mughal court designs of the 17th century, but have continued to be popular ever since. Such 'flat' decoration has often been preferred to the realistic pattern. This block-printed and dyed example comes from Rajastan.

**Silk, England, c.1776–8**
A pretty brocaded satin fabric intended to be used for ladies' gowns. The technique of brocading enabled different colours to be introduced into the pattern of a fabric, often in very small areas. Although the method is labour intensive, it produces intricate patterning.

**Cotton, Britain, 1934**
Apparently random motifs floating on a plain ground were particularly fashionable in the 1930s. This example is a crêpe fabric printed with a repeat of leaves in complementary red and light pinks, on a dark blue background.

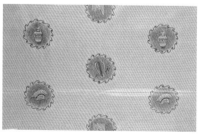

**Satin, Britain, 1947**
Designed by Lucienne Day, the pattern of this furnishing fabric reflects her enthusiasm for simple shapes, but with an element of conversational interest, achieved by placing small images of iconic Ancient Greek objects into a basic offset repeat of circles with wavy edges.

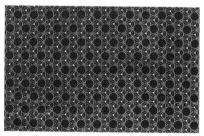

**Silk, detail, England, 1951**
The British Festival Pattern Group developed motifs taken from the crystalline structure of different substances into textile patterns. This fabric, called 'China Clay', shows the symmetrical arrangement of one crystal, making it particularly suitable for adaptation into a small repeat.

# Large Repeats

### 17th–20th Century

Large, regular repeats are one of the classic forms for textiles. They occur in a wide variety of shapes and sizes, but are generally based on some type of grid, which might be triangular, pentagonal or square in basic outline. The pattern within large repeats also often uses areas that mirror motifs, either up and down or side to side. The repeats may be naturalistic or geometric, employ 'island' patterns or showcase major motifs joined by trailing features: the key feature is their scale. Large repeats lend themselves particularly to applications as hangings or curtains, where there is a long drop of fabric to show them off successfully.

**Velvet, England, early 17th century**

A superb embroidered pulpit hanging, featuring a large and intricate mirrored pattern design. It shows a winged, angel-like figure surrounded by tendrils of foliage, and is probably derived from Renaissance arabesques, which favoured symmetrically intertwining foliage punctuated by set-piece motifs.

**Design for fabric, England, 1897**

This textile pattern by the architect and designer A.W.N. Pugin demonstrates the principles he laid down for a new Victorian aesthetic that preferred stylisation to naturalistic designs. The pentagon shape may represent a stylised mitre; Pugin undertook a substantial amount of work for the Catholic Church.

**Silk, England, late 19th century**

In 1856 Owen Jones published *The Grammar of Ornament*, an analysis of patterns and colours from many periods and different cultures. Jones thought that reproducing flowers in a naturalistic way was tasteless. He preferred stylised motifs, as this example with a loose 'diamond' theme demonstrates.

**Wool and cotton, Scotland, late 19th century**

Named 'Omar', possibly after *The Rubáiyát of Omar Khayyám*, this Jacquard weave features a repeating ogival pattern of tulips and leaves, reminiscent of 16th- and 17th-century Turkish velvets. It was designed by the architect Charles Harrison Townsend.

**Design for lace, Scotland, 2008**

This design by Timorous Beasties, aptly entitled 'Devil Damask', has its origins in the damasks of the Renaissance period. The mirrored pattern around a central axis is also reminiscent of Hermann Rorschach's inkblot tests, created in 1921, which are used for psychological evaluations.

# Boteh

### 19th Century

Much speculation surrounds the origins of the Eastern *boteh* or pine motif from which the paisley pattern is derived. *Boteh* is a Persian word for a flowering shrub, and it seems probable that the pattern originated in ancient Babylon, where a teardrop shape was used to characterise the growing shoot of a date palm. The many benefits of the palm encouraged it to be seen as a 'Tree of Life', while its sprouting shoot was used as a fertility symbol as well. The popularity of the original Kashmiri shawls featuring *boteh* motifs encouraged European imitations (*see pages 116–17*).

**Cashmere, Kashmir, early 19th century**
A woven shawl that demonstrates how patterns can be built up using various scales and treatments. The larger *boteh* motifs make up the main body of the pattern, whilst the smaller ones are laid at 45 degrees as a border.

**Cashmere, detail, Kashmir, mid 19th century**
In this woven shawl scale is again used to define the pattern, as in the example shown on the left. The larger motifs are for the body of the pattern; the scaled-down versions are laid at 90 degrees, making a very attractive border.

**Wool, detail, Kashmir, 19th century**

The corner of a woven shawl showing a large paisley-type motif with an extended hanging tip, and a border of palmette (stylised palm leaf) foliage. The pear shape or *boteh* can be rendered in many subtly different ways.

**Pashmina, detail, Kashmir, 19th century**

The finest shawls have designs woven on a loom. although many examples from the 1830s onwards duplicated these woven designs in embroidery. because it was easier and quicker to make. This example has very elongated motifs that are still clearly recognisable as *boteh*.

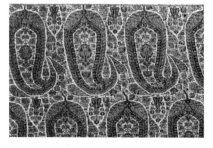

**Cashmere, Kashmir, late 19th century**

Not all Kashmiri material was made into shawls. This woven dress piece exhibits a very busy design of infill pattern as a background to the larger pear forms, which themselves are made up from two differing outlines that emphasise the traditional teardrop shape.

# Paisley

## 16th–19th century

The patterns now universally known as 'paisley' are based on the motifs found on woven shawls originally imported from India (*see pages 114–15*). Rich, curvilinear, highly stylised floral forms, along with a particular motif that makes them instantly recognisable, characterise the pattern. The motif most strongly associated with paisley is the comma-shaped pear (*boteh*) or kidney. Introduced into Europe in the first half of the 17th century, paisley and other Indian patterns were hugely popular. However, in the 19th century European production of these designs became important, particularly in the Scottish town of Paisley, which ultimately lent its name to the *boteh* motif and its associated patterns.

**Silk, Ottoman Empire, late 16th/early 17th century**
A cushion cover of silk embroidered in *atma* (combination stitch) and couched metal threads (outlines). The blue ground is decorated with offset medallions, each with a small 'root' at the bottom and two leaves at the top, which are very similar in form to the *boteh*.

**Design for fabric, England, 19th century**
A pattern by George Charles Haite, who
published a book of shawl designs, featuring
an intricate *boteh* shape that is completely
filled in with smaller decorative motifs.
The development of the Jacquard loom
enabled Europeans to produce woven work
that began to approach the quality of the
Kashmiri originals.

**Design for fabric, England, 19th century**
This repeat pattern, another by George
Charles Haite, features a heavily stylised
paisley motif, with jagged edges surrounded
and separated by intertwining flowers. The
whole illustrates the potential flexibility
and adaptability of the basic paisley shape.

**Silk fragment,
England,
c. 1850–80**
A small piece of
Jacquard-woven
dress fabric, which
features an
abstracted paisley
pattern outline on
a red background.
This rather spare
and unusual pattern
demonstrates how a
designer can take
the essentials of a
form and abstract it
into something that
is novel and
distinctive.

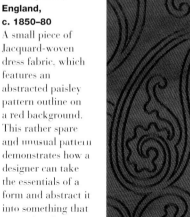

**Cotton, India, c.1880s**
A detail of a print showing a conventional,
regular repeat of the *boteh* form, achieved
by a combination of printing with wooden
blocks and hand-painting with a *kalam*
(Persian for 'pen') tool. The latter gives this
type of textile, from the south of India, the
generic name of *kalamkari* ('pen work').

# Roundels & Rosettes

### Ancient to Modern

A roundel is any circular shape that encloses a pattern, whereas a rosette is a round, stylised flower design; both are used extensively in pattern-making. In the 4th and 5th centuries AD, they were common elements in Egyptian patterns and have remained favourites ever since. They are useful as dividing mechanisms, as well as acting as frame around vignettes, or smaller self-contained designs. Roundels are sometimes referred to as medallions because of their similarity in shape. They appear in patterns across cultures and time periods, so are part of many long-standing traditions.

**Silk, Persian Empire, 600–1000**

A woven panel featuring roundels enclosing paired lions, with paired foxes and hounds below, which demonstrates the use of this form as a framing device. The Persian taste for paired or facing creatures reflects an interest in symmetry and geometry.

**Silk, Persia, 8th–9th century**

A woven twill decorated with a *senmurv* in a pearl-bordered roundel. The *senmurv* (or *simurgh*) is a Persian mythological beast, with similar qualities to a griffin, and is often represented as a combination of a bird and either a dog or a lion.

**Silk, Italy, 1270–1399**
Ornamented with gold thread, this woven panel features roundels containing paired griffins, impressive mythological creatures which had the heads and wings of eagles allied to the bodies of lions – powerful subjects for the designer to work with.

**Silk, Turkey, 1550–1600**
This Ottoman woven textile is of the type known in Turkish as a *seraser*, which refers to a cloth faced all over with gold or silver thread. Here the silver ground has a prominent pattern of roundels worked in red and green, and set in rows.

**Silk, Ottoman Empire, 17th century**
Some Ottoman textiles were decorated with medallion-shaped compartments, often combined with delicate lattices at this date. In this cushion cover, the designer has discarded the lattice and only the medallions remain.

# Roundels & Rosettes

**Cotton, detail, Japan, 19th century**

Roundels feature in this cotton futon cover, or *futon-ji*, with paste-resist decoration. The roundel here depicts an elaborate curving fish, but the whole piece is adorned with various circles and roundels that contain a variety of stylised plants or birds, or are sometimes simple ornamental geometric forms.

**Silk and paper, detail, Japan, 19th century**

A beautifully fresh-looking brocaded altar cloth featuring gold-wrapped paper details, and with additional applied pattern. The pale background is made up of a geometric lattice and the vertical bamboo lengths are overlaid with roundels and stylised leaves.

**Lace, detail, Flanders, c.1800**

A corner of a bobbin-lace veil featuring linked roundels, in a pattern known as a *guilloche*, derived from classical architecture and consisting of two or more bands intertwined to form a continuous row of connected circles.

**Silk, detail, Japan, mid 19th century**

A satin kimono with silk embroidery featuring floral roundels, this garment would have been worn by a woman of the samurai class. In Japan the pink azalea symbolises family devotion, because the blossoms flower close to the parent stem.

**Lace, detail, England, c.1862**

This decorated roundel with a picture of flowers in the centre is part of a finely worked Honiton flounce, its delicate gauze-like background contrasting with the open work around the outside of the motif. Natural forms were popular in the Honiton work of the 1860s.

# Oriental Carpets

### 16th–17th Century

Featuring endlessly inventive stylised patterns, oriental carpets have given inspiration to Western designers ever since they were widely imported to Europe in the 15th century. Patterns may be rooted in symbolism or geometry or both. Numerous different motifs are found in Eastern carpets, but the ones most commonly seen are the Tree of Life, pomegranates, camels, dogs, peacocks, doves and cockerels. Colour is also used to represent states of being – brown indicates fertility, for example, and red, happiness.

**Carpet, Persia, 16th century**
Known as the 'Chelsea' carpet because it was bought from a dealer in Chelsea, this well known piece has a main field containing two large compositions of big and small medallions, balanced by the central motif of two vases of flowers placed on either side of a pond. The compactly decorated field and border include many different animals.

**Carpet, fragment, Persia, 16th century**
A hand-knotted woollen pile on a silk warp
and wool-and-silk weft. Although the pairs
of fighting animals are barely larger than
some of the flowers, they contain vivid
details and repay close examination.

**Carpet, Turkey, 16th–17th century**
Pieces with this distinctive yellow and red
design are often called Lotto carpets because
the 16th-century Italian artist Lorenzo Lotto
depicted them in his paintings. The designs
were made up from prepared drawings, so it
was easy to change the proportions of the
carpet by selecting parts of the design.

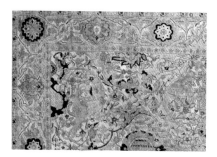

**Carpet, detail, Persia, early 17th century**
The brocaded metal threads used to
enhance this hand-knotted silk and wool
carpet help to highlight the elaborately
intertwined nature of the pattern, which
has resonances with Islamic architectural
decoration and with calligraphy.

**Carpet, Persia, 17th century**
Made during the Safavid dynasty in Persia,
this carpet features motifs organised in a
lattice pattern in various ways. They reflect
the style that developed later, which was
characterised by symmetrical scrollwork
designs set with fantastic blossoms. William
Morris once owned this piece.

# Kimonos

### 19th–20th Century

Kimonos are the traditional garment of Japan, simple, straight-seamed, worn wrapped left side over right and secured with a sash called an *obi*. The length of the garment can be altered for height by drawing up excess fabric under the *obi*, while other adjustments can be made to suit the wearer. The surface patterning in kimonos is significant, as it indicates personal identity, status and cultural awareness, all key in the extremely hierarchical social structure of Japan.

**Silk, detail, Japan, 1870–90**
This figured fabric ornamented with paste-resist (*yuzen*) and metallic thread embroidery has a stylised pattern entitled 'Rippling Water, Bamboo and Birds' – all typical Japanese motifs associated with nature and the seasons.

**Silk, Japan, 19th century**
An impressive pattern of cranes, pine trees, clouds and chrysanthemums has been created with stencils and bright mineral pigments, using the *bingata* technique. Only members of the Ryukyuan royal family wore robes such as this.

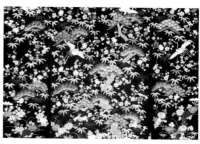

**Silk, detail, Japan, late 19th century**
A sumptuous overall design of auspicious motifs of pine, bamboo, plum, peony, chrysanthemum, crane and tortoise is embroidered on to a crêpe base. This type of kimono was often exported to the West in the late 19th century in response to the growing fashion for Japanese objects.

**Silk, detail, Japan, 1912–15**
The main element of this design is bamboo, which in Japan, is considered one of the three trees of good omen. In its height – reaching for the sky – and its straightness, bamboo is also used to symbolise the character of Buddhist and Tao meditation.

**Silk, detail, Japan, c.1970**
Designed for a young woman, this figured silk with applied printed decoration features traditional motifs, including open fans, flowers, ribbons and leaves linked by a meandering stream, all transformed into a vivid psychedelic design. The brilliant colours give the pattern a very modern effect.

# Introduction

The use of geometric shapes is a very obvious way of making repeating patterns. Any geometric shape can either be manipulated to create an interesting repeat on its own or used in conjunction with other pattern types to create a different form of tessellation. They may have symbolic qualities, they may be a framework for another design or they may be artistic representations, but the way that they combine is key to the harmony of patterns. Whatever their purpose, geometric shapes seem to go to the very heart of pattern-making.

**Rug, Persia, 19th century**
Woven with camel-hair pile on cotton warp and woollen weft, this piece has a typically Persian motif of a central medallion. Most Kashan rugs follow a medallion-and-spandrel or corner-design pattern, also known as a book-cover or Koran design, in reference to the tooled leather covers used to bind the Koran.

**Silk, Spain, 14th century**
An Islamic-inspired woven pattern in which each design unit contains an eight-pointed star, a quatrefoil and two roundels. The compartments they form are filled with a variety of smaller motifs, from interlaced patterns in green or blue to tiny knots and fleurs-de-lys.

**Cotton, detail, England, c.1804–10**
A curtain in classically influenced
Pompeian colours, featuring a main field
of small repeating motifs surrounded by
a straight-line border, sub-divided into
several rows, including a line of circles
and a castellated pattern with a variety
of motifs in each of its notches.

**Silk, probably France, c.1925**
A printed scarf with a repeating motif
of interlocking L-shapes, each shape
composed of three lines. A bold horizontal
black line divides the pattern in half.
The neat, sharply angled design is
characteristic of the Art Deco period.

**Cotton, England, 1962**
A screen-printed furnishing fabric entitled
'Reciprocation', designed by Barbara
Brown for Heal Fabrics. One of two
intended to be used together, this is on a
slightly smaller scale than its partner and is
made up of alternating squares and circles,
the most basic of geometric designs.

# Zigzags

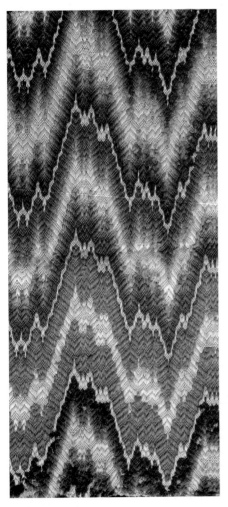

### 17th–20th Century

Zigzags are forms produced by lines laid at variable angles, which remain constant within the pattern. A zigzag can be described as both pointed and regular; the 'zig' is the line pointing to the left and the 'zag' is that pointing to the right. For the pattern-maker, a symmetrical design can be produced by mirroring a segment of a zigzag line for as long as required in repeat. V-shaped chevrons can also be juxtaposed so that they line up and make the pattern. There is little specific symbolism attached to this very basic repeating pattern, although the zigzag 'flash' is sometimes used to represent lightning.

### Embroidered canvas, Italy, c.1650–99

Silk and wool are used here in a dense flame stitch, covering the ground fabric with an irregular zigzag pattern in striped shades of brown, yellow and dark green. This is a good example of how the zigzag can be distorted to create a less regimented effect.

**Silk, detail, Japan, 1750–1850**
This brocade robe shows something of the beauty of the *No* theatre costumes, using a combination of natural-coloured chrysanthemums and a stylised circle placed on a lattice background: a version of the zigzag that creates a trellis effect.

**Wool, Central Asia (Beluch), 19th century**
The ornamentation of an *ok-bash*, or spindle bag, is made up from a field of bands of zigzags, with a main border of linked floral motifs, and inner and outer borders with bands of interlocking Y-motifs extending along both sides of the piece.

**Cotton, Pakistan, mid 19th century**
Part of a woman's dress or *pushk*, beautifully and carefully embroidered with silk. The regular repeated chevrons dominate the design, while the smaller cone shapes and crosses provide edging and infill. The chevrons themselves are highlighted with smaller stitches.

# Zigzags

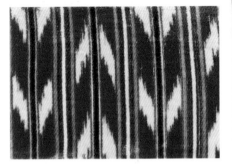

**Velvet, fragment, Japan, late 19th century**
Mounted in an album, this fabric is woven with selectively pre-dyed yarns called *kasuri* (a weft-ikat technique). The zigzag pattern is overlaid with striped bands, creating a chevron effect.

**Cotton, detail, India, 19th century**
A vibrant turban cloth from Rajasthan, an area well known for the brilliant colours of its women's clothes. This piece is equally vivid, tie-dyed in black, yellow and white zigzags.

**Linen, England, 1922**
A printed furnishing fabric designed by Gregory Brown, featuring a classic Art Deco geometric design of chevrons overlaid with zigzags. The zigzag was popular in the 1920s and featured in many aspects of architecture and design.

**Linen and cotton, detail, England, 1930**
A furnishing fabric designed by the
St Edmundsbury Weavers and produced by
the Edinburgh Weavers company. Its torch-
like image is based on the linked zigzags
and fan outlines that are characteristic of
the geometric patterns of the period.

**Yarn and corded cotton, England, 1946**
A simple but attractive woven furnishing
fabric designed by Enid Marx for the
Utility Design Panel, a government
organisation responsible for producing
good quality designs within rigid
economical constraints.

**Velvet, England, 2008**
Entitled 'Zebra', this woven cloth is
designed by Neisha Crosland. Despite its
apparent bold simplicity, the pattern is quite
complex, with two-directional zigzags filled
by smaller triangles placed at different
angles. The viewer can see spearheads,
pointing up, and icicles, pointing down.

# Squares

### 19th–20th Century

The square is amongst the most basic of geometric shapes. It is rich in symbolism as it is often used to represent the mathematical and scientific order of the universe. In its two-dimensional nature it may symbolise the earth or the ground, or, more specifically, a field, especially in Eastern imagery. In Buddhist symbolism, the square within the circle represents the relationship of the human and the divine. In Christian symbolism, a square represents spiritual notions related to the number four, such as the four corners of the Earth and the four evangelists.

**Silk, detail, Japan, 19th century**

The *hitatare* was the robe of a samurai, often decorated with a crest. This brocaded example features blue and silver floral roundels on a green and cream squared chequerboard ground. The combination of the ghostly circles and the rigid squares makes for an arresting effect.

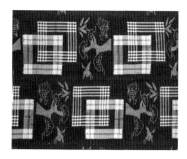

**Cotton, detail, Japan, 19th century**

This bedding cover is woven with selectively pre-dyed yarns (*kasuri*) and a complex pattern of auspicious symbols of pine trees, tortoise and crane with an overlaid design of squares. The piece is a superb example of the successful combination of natural forms and geometric shapes.

**Cotton, Japan, 19th–20th century**

A blue and white cover for a futon which is characteristically patterned with propitious motifs alternating with a bold geometric pattern of inlaid squares. The design was created by means of *kasuri*, a technique in which certain sections of the yarn to be woven are bound before being dyed.

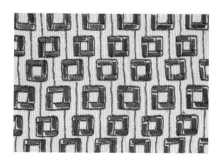

**Linen, England, 1913**

'Mechtilde', a printed furnishing fabric, by the Omega Workshops, with a regular pattern of thick squares, each made up of four rectangular blocks. The piece is probably an abstracted take on the story of the 13th-century St Mechtilde, who wrote her visions down on separate sheets of paper.

**Cotton and rayon, England, 1935**

Designed by T. Bradley for Allan Walton Textiles, a company that embraced the ethos of the Industrial Art Movement in its designs. This printed furnishing textile has a pattern of slightly eccentric overlaid squares that link to each other. The result is a grid-like maze effect.

# Polygons

### 18th–20th Century

Polygons are closed figures consisting of straight-line segments, which form the sides of the shape. Regular polygonal shapes are frequently seen in nature, especially in the mineral world. They occur in many ways in textile patterns, in every imaginable application, and are successfully used as a simple way of creating a regular repeat. The hexagon and the octagon are particularly popular on everything from carpets to hangings. Polygons are often symbolic of sacred ideas, or geometry and number relationships.

**(Unknown), Greece, 18th century**
In Christian iconography the octagon represents salvation, symbolising the eighth day, when Christ reappeared to his disciples after his resurrection. The use of octagonal panels alongside geometric floral motifs embroidered on this bed curtain from the Cyclades, may have symbolic importance.

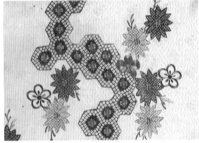

**Silk, detail, Japan, 1750–1800**
The figured fabric of this piece, which features tie-dyed (*shibori*), stencilled (*katakanoko*) as well as embroidered decoration, has a neat, confident pattern that juxtaposes geometric elements – hexagons – and natural ones – flowers.

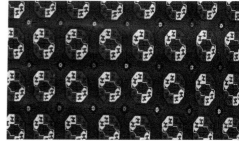

**Carpet, detail, Turkmenistan, 19th century**

In many carpets from western Central Asia, octagons are the main motif. In this piece, probably made by the Yomud tribal group, the octagons are used boldly in a simple repeating pattern, each divided into contrasting quarters of different colours.

**Wool, Sweden, 19th century**

The banded geometric pattern on this wall hanging, with lozenges, stars, stripes and stylised plant life, is representative of traditional craftwork in the Skane region. This pattern makes use of the stepped sides of polygons in a range of scales.

**Wool, England, 1973**

A mixture of geometric shapes is juxtaposed in this Jacquard-woven furnishing fabric. Small diamond shapes are made up of tiny squares, and are laid onto a square grid background that itself metamorphoses into a series of polygons. The eye can also perceive a criss-cross effect over the whole.

# Diamonds

### 17th–20th Century

In geometry a rhombus (from the ancient Greek word for a spinning top) is a four-sided polygon in which every side has the same length, and in design and pattern terms, the rhombus is more commonly called a diamond (after the suit in the card deck), or a lozenge. For textile designers the diamond is another simple geometric shape that can be adapted to create lively patterns and which is also easy to use in repeats.

**Carpet, detail, Norway, 17th century**
A dramatic pattern of jagged diaper shapes created by a flat-weave technique shows how simple patterns can create bold designs. The mechanical repetition of motifs is typical of these simple home-crafted products. It is often the case that diamond shapes create secondary patterns – in this particular case, a grid – by default.

**Silk lined with leather, England, 1628**
A purse decorated with glass beads, used to create the repeated pattern of an 'S' within a small diamond trellis in white, black, yellow and turquoise on a ground of brown. The ground is filled with an outline trellis design.

**Carpet, Persia, 19th century**
This piece, hand-knotted in wool on a woollen warp and weft, originated in Azerbaijan and offers a good example of a balanced, confident and lively pattern. A central row of three concentric hexagons reflects the diaper-pattern base of diamond shapes.

**Cotton, China, 20th century**
Featuring white motifs on a blue ground, this panel of resist-dyed fabric contains a main framework of diamonds, each of which contains circles and curlicues. Diagonal lines of dots control the effect and the whole is framed in a rectangle outlined with dots and circles.

**Cotton, China, 20th century**
A distinctive textile that makes its impact with strong colours and a small twist in scale: each of the white diamonds is broken up into four smaller forms with dark-red detailing, then set on a tan background in which each motif seems to be part of another, larger diamond.

# Trellis

### 14th–20th Century

The term trellis indicates a framework made up from vertical and horizontal strips, or from crossed diagonal strips; in its original form it described the structure used to support climbing plants. Designers have long since appropriated the form, and later the word, to use both as a support within climbing floral patterns or, more loosely, to be abstracted into other patterns. The value of a trellis (also called a lattice) in pattern-making is its flexibility: it can remain as a simple abstract geometric form, can be adorned naturalistically or can be used as a framework for other images.

**Silk, Germany, 14th century**

An early embroidered bag with a trellis pattern that creates spaces to hold a variety of symbols from Christian iconography, including a pelican pecking its breast, a symbol of the Cross and the letter M. These indicate that the bag was used for religious purposes.

**Wool and cotton, Persia, 19th century**

*Soumak* is a decorative stitch in which the thread is wrapped around each warp, usually on a diagonal, to create a herring-bone effect. This saddlebag uses a woollen warp and a cotton weft, and is decorated with a trellis effect made up from small diamonds, each filled with typically Persian carpet motifs.

**Cotton, England, c.1878–80**

This dense and elaborate pattern has two completely separate elements. The complex geometric bands that make up the trellis effect are overlaid with a lavish repeat of bunches of *Syringa vulgaris*, a lilac with strongly veined and heart-shaped green leaves that offers a lively and successful contrast with the more formal ground.

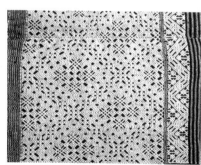

**Ramie, detail, Japan, late 19th–early 20th century**

The style of this indigo-dyed ramie fabric, stitched in white cotton (*kogin*) is specific to women living in Tsugaru, in the very north of Honshu. The diamond design is as distinctive as the production method. The fabric is part of a kimono.

**(Unknown), Britain, 1949**

Designed by the eminent Swiss-born weaver Marianne Straub for Helios Ltd, the simple but subtle lozenge shapes on this woven furnishing fabric reflect a taste for restrained Modernism. The design recalls those that Straub was commissioned to design for the London Underground.

# Waves

### 20th Century

Wave forms, although associated with water and the sea, are usually stylised in textile design, and are often created from two partial circles arranged to form a wavy line with fillets placed on either side. The concave and convex lines create a loose S-shape, sometimes called a *cyma recta*. Waves can have a different symbolic impact on the onlooker, depending on whether they identify with someone caught and made helpless by the water's strength – promoting a feeling of inevitability and passivity – or see the waves as representing the uncontrollable power of the sea.

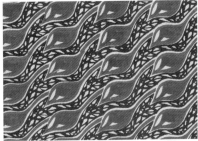

**Wool and linen, England, 1913**
A Jacquard-woven furnishing fabric, 'Cracow', designed and sold by the avant-garde Omega Workshops whose aim was to bring the richness of contemporary fine art to everyday things. This material was advertised for sale as a hard-wearing tapestry for upholstery use.

**Cotton, Scotland, c.1918**
Designed by the architect Charles Rennie Mackintosh, this printed furnishing fabric features motifs similar to leaves, but the end effect is of waves moving across the material. Mackintosh is best known for his furniture and interiors, and this design is from a late stage in his career.

## Cotton and rayon, England, 1932

A screen-printed furnishing fabric designed by H.J. Bull for Allan Walton Textiles, which demonstrates a strong rhythmic composition that juxtaposes straight edges and curves. The abstract geometry and the powerful, balanced impression left by this example are typical of the period.

## Cotton, England, 1934

Charles Grant, the designer of this pattern for a Jacquard weave called 'Mendip', uses it to explore the S-shapes of a wave against a structured background. The thinner darker line is set up in contrast to the thicker grey wave, creating an interesting tension between forms.

## Silk, detail, Japan, 1973

'Green Waves', a kimono fabric with an abstract pattern, is made using a rice-paste resist-dyed decoration called *yuzen*. The green quarter-circles represent a wave, giving the design a modern, slightly disjointed appearance – but note that one continuous wave-line crosses the fabric diagonally, linking the different elements.

# Circles

### 19th–20th Century

Circles are among the most elementary of geometric images, but carry some of the greatest symbolic strength. The circle is one of four fundamental symbols (the others being the centre, the cross and the square). Its completeness is often used to convey infinity, as the ultimate and perfect geometric shape. The circle has been used in myriad ways in every art and design form, and its endless versatility has made it a popular choice for textile designers.

**Silk, detail, Japan, 19th century**

A twill-weave temple altar cloth with brocaded silk and gold and wrapped paper decoration depicting chrysanthemum roundels and scrolling leaves. In Japan, the chrysanthemum, the autumn flower, is both a symbol of the sun and the emblem of the royal family, who are believed to be descended from the sun god.

**Wool and cotton, England, c.1845**
A woven curtain, designed by A.W.N. Pugin,
and shown at the Great Exhibition of 1851.
Reminiscent of medieval patterning, which
was based on compass work, it uses a linked
pattern of circles and fleurs-de-lys or a strict
repeat of fleurs-de-lys surrounded by smaller
motifs, depending on how you view it.

**Silk, detail, India, late 19th century**
This skirt is made of satin weave and
embroidered with silk threads. The pattern
is of circular stylised flower heads in black
and red on a cream background, laid out in
a regular repeat. The finely stitched border,
typical of Kutch work from Gujarat, has a
design of parrots, flowers and shells.

**Silk, China,
19th–20th century**
Subdued twill roundels
featuring elaborately
drawn dragons are
woven along the full
length of this light
yellow material.
The dragon image,
a symbol of the
emperor, has long
been associated with
China. This type of
pattern lends itself well
to east-Asian straight-
seamed tailoring work.

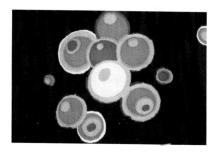

**Cotton, England, 1920**
The pattern on this furnishing fabric is
based on a contrast between the vertical
stripes in dark colours and the lighter-
toned circles, themselves filled with smaller
circles, overlaying them. The purple and
orange colouring is typical of the vivid hues
of contemporary designs.

# Optical Illusions

## 20th Century

This group of fabrics from the 20th century exhibits the continuing fascination with optical illusions. Op Art, a movement in the fine arts particularly preoccupied with visual trickery and was extremely popular in the 1960s, was one source of inspiration for textile patterns. Most of these designs are abstract, and many of the best-known images were only produced in black and white. When looked at, they seem to move, vibrate, advance or retreat. They work particularly well used as hangings or curtains: a long, vertical drop increases the illusory image and further confounds the eye.

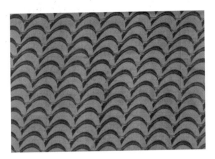

**Silk, Scotland, 1918**
A dress fabric designed by Charles Rennie Mackintosh, which produces a stunningly three-dimensional effect by the simple means of offsetting a repeated semicircle at an angle. The result may be read as scales, roof tiles, shells or overlapping arches.

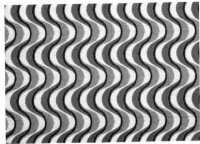

**Cotton and wool, Holland, c.1930**
A dynamic pattern in the abstract and muted colours that were growing in popularity during the 1930s. Made as a hanging, designed by Jean Bouzois, the piece has a vibrant design similar to the Op Art patterns of the late 1960s.

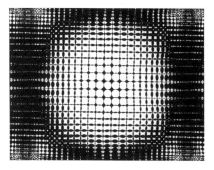

**Cotton, England, 1965**

'Impact', a screenprinted sateen furnishing fabric by Evelyn Brooks for Heal Fabrics, makes obvious references to Op Art. The relationship between illusion and surface is evident, and the black and white colour scheme is also a strong link to the fine art of the time.

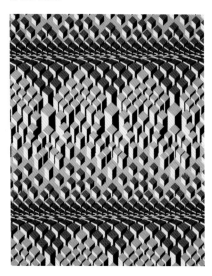

**Cotton, England, 1966**

The psychedelic black and white imagery that draws the eye in and out of this screenprinted furnishing fabric, designed by Barbara Brown for Heal Fabrics, is typical of the 1960s and would be especially effective hung as curtains.

**Cotton, Britain, 1973**

The design of regular shaded blocks resembling buildings in a city is echoed by the name of this printed furnishing fabric: 'Metropolis'. It can also, though, be seen as a purely abstract pattern, with all the tricks and distortions characteristic of Op Art fabrics.

ABSTRACT

# Introduction

Abstract designs for textiles, as for many other objects, span the gamut of artistic production from ancient times to contemporary work. They can be divided into those that are abstractions of real forms and those that are pure, unreferenced invention. In early and less-developed cultures, designs and marks based on simple, geometric and linear forms may have had a symbolic or decorative purpose, no longer clear to the contemporary viewer. In any event, it is their visual impact rather than any hidden meaning for which abstract designs are valued. This selection looks at a cross-section of abstract patterns to demonstrate the full range and variety of shapes and colours used.

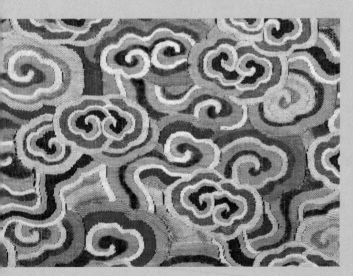

**Silk, detail, China, early 19th century**
An interlinked pattern of swirls on this woven dragon robe are arranged in a design that appears random. The swirling motifs may actually represent highly abstracted clouds, which in Chinese tradition stand for the dissolving of a perishable being before reaching eternity.

**Silk and cotton, detail, Central Asia, mid 19th century**

Ikat dyeing, a speciality of the cities of Uzbekistan, is a resist-dyeing technique in which the warp threads (and sometimes the wefts) are tie-dyed to create the pattern before the fabric is woven. The patterns here may be symbolic or simply pleasing.

**Silk and wool, England, c.1870**

A woven furnishing fabric, by Edward William Godwin, based on Japanese abstract *komai* patterns in which areas of geometrical pattern are divided by straight edges or lines. This example looks rather mechanical compared to the organic flow of the Japanese originals.

**Design for fabric, USA, c.1940–50**

An abstract pattern for use in dress fabric which bears all the hallmarks of the mid 20th-century period. It is painterly in its casual effect, which is achieved by imitating the rough brushstrokes and dabs of speedy artwork. Executed in gouache on paper, the design is ready to be transferred to cloth.

**Cotton, Britain, 1952**

A screenprinted crêpe by Marian Mahler for David Whitehead Ltd. The abstract pattern here is based on a swinging mobile – a sculptural form that was popular in the 1940s and 50s. By transferring a three-dimensional design to a flat pattern, it has become more abstract.

# Patchwork

### 18th–19th Century

Patchwork is generally developed using repeat patterns built up with different-coloured geometric shapes cut from a selection of textiles. Stitched together they form a larger design that may be random or regular. Originally employed as a thrifty way of using scraps, patchwork gained status as an art in its own right; some pieces display areas of fabric specially chosen for the purpose. Specific effects can be created, such as chequerboards, star shapes or colour sliding that goes from light to dark and vice versa. Although widely used in many cultures, patchwork is especially closely associated with England and North America.

**Patchwork, England, mid 18th century**
Probably worked by Mary Parker, this fine example of the craft uses simple triangles as the basic pattern shapes. The variety of fabrics used here creates different effects within the pattern, so that the viewer sees hourglass shapes, squares and diamond outlines in addition to the triangle form.

**Patchwork, England, c.1760s**

A piece made up of dress silks and ribbons, lined with printed cottons, in a basic range of geometric shapes. The main pattern is overlaid with bands and bordered, giving it a more structured appearance. The four corners have enlarged versions of the small detail in the field.

**Patchwork, detail, England, late 18th century**

An overlapping shell or scale pattern with a mirror repeat of the printed and painted cottons included gives this quilt an underlying structure, while the main work is divided into much larger diamonds by scalloped bands.

**Patchwork, England, 1875**

A cover of coloured silks and felts that offers a general outline of the story of a couple, from first courting to old age. Each vignette displays a typical part of a Victorian love story and matrimony, generalised to make sense to all.

**Patchwork, England, 1895**

Pieced from a variety of plain satin and printed silk dress fabrics. There does not appear to be any order to the work on this quilt – the pattern is random and abstract – but the overall balance of shapes and colours is effective.

# Painterly

### 20th Century

During the early 20th century a number of well-known artists tried their hand at pattern-making for textiles. This development, often in conjunction with the rise of abstraction in modern painting, was also reflected in commercial patterns of the time. The similarity of a flat canvas and a flat textile ready for printing is clear. The combination of abstract forms and geometry, often with a very lively working of the shapes and colours within a design, represented a 'modern' approach to patterning that was revolutionary.

**Cotton, France, early 20th century**
Designed by the Art Deco artist Madame Andrada, this furnishing fabric of printed cotton exhibits an exuberant abstract but regular pattern featuring various geometric shapes in assorted warm bright colours, and including a black and white chequerboard pattern.

**Linen, England, 1913**

'Amenophis', a furnishing fabric, was produced by Roger Fry for the Omega Workshops. Their innovative textile designs set a fashion for abstract and geometric themes. The pattern here is based on Fry's painting *Still Life with Eggs and Books*.

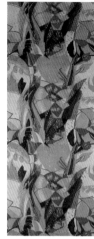

**Cotton, England, c.1920s**

A roller-printed furnishing fabric designed by Minnie McLeish for William Foxton Ltd. McLeish was known for bold, bright patterns that owe something to the influence of Cubist painters, in this case visible particularly in the central column of heavily abstracted flowers.

**Silk, France, c. 1920s**

The influence of fine painters on decorative art in France at this time was very strong, and many artists worked as designers as well. In this example, the influence of the Fauves and their bold colour schemes is combined with an exotic image of a stylised woman with a turban.

**Cotton, England, 1923**

This roller-printed furnishing fabric features a painterly palette of colours reflecting contemporary art, within an abstract geometric pattern of rectangular planes. Each rectangle is decorated with zigzag patterns comprising a multitude of different colours.

# Spirals

### 19th–21st Century

To make patterns using spirals is to press into service a motif that is found in most cultures, and which has been used since ancient times. The spiral may be helical or flat. In its flat form it is most like a maze, evolving from a point, then falling back to the centre. By contrast, the helical shape reflects the repetitive rhythm of life and the cycle of evolution. Symbolically, the spiral has represented the moon and also been linked to aquatic fertility.

**Design for fabric, France, 1890**
A systematic and neat repeat of a spiral pattern ornaments this design for dress fabric, creating rows of figure-of-eight motifs. The image brings to mind old-fashioned braiding or gimp trimming, and may have been intended to reproduce that effect, while the shading on the pattern gives the impression of a metallic finish.

**Cotton, Japan, 19th century**
A futon cover with *rasuri* (resist-dyed) decoration that incorporates two of the major traditional symbols of Japan. The chrysanthemums symbolise the sun and represent longevity, whilst the spiralling shapes may be interpreted as waves or clouds bringing auspicious omens.

## Rug, England, c.1936

Designed by Marion Dorn for the Wilton Royal Carpet Factory in Art Deco style, this example has a large ribbon spiral overlaid with stylised ears of corn. Dorn's work was mainly abstract and included volutes, spirals, zigzags and other geometric motifs.

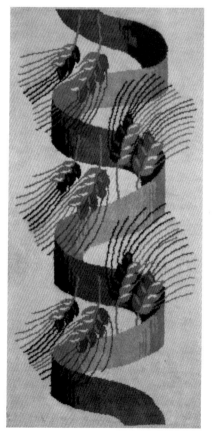

## Cotton, England, 1969

A screen-printed furnishing fabric designed by Barbara Brown for Heal Fabrics. The huge scale of the pattern is quite unusual and can be interpreted as an architectural form, a highly formalised column, or something less traditional such as a helter skelter, or even a massively enlarged screw.

## Linen, England, 2008

A delightfully inventive printed design offering a form that is a cross between a spiral and a wave. Neisha Crosland's 'Hedgehog' pattern uses a wavy line that is embellished with various-sized spines to create a slightly unsettling pattern of continuous loops of spikes or quills.

# Art Deco

### 20th Century

The period of design known as Art Deco, which lasted from the beginning of the 1920s into the 1930s, has a particular resonance in the history of abstract patterning. It is characterised by an eclectic amalgam of elegant and stylish modern design that was influenced by a wide range of sources. Amongst them were the so-called 'primitive' arts of Africa, ancient Egypt, and Central and South America, as well as contemporary imagery drawn from technology and architecture. Cubism and Futurism were also influential during this rich decade of design.

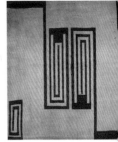

**Pochoir bookplate, detail, France, 1930**
Best known as a fashion designer and decorator, Paul Poiret conceived this pattern for furnishing fabric. Although the abstraction of the trees and leaves is representative of the period, it is the dog motif that is most typical. In the example, the dog is shown as both elegant and swift.

**Carpet, England, c.1930s**
The flattened Modernist spiral design on this piece may have been inspired by the Parisian carpet designer Ivan da Silva Bruhns. There are echoes of South American ethnic styles in this work, which are also characteristic of his particular style.

**Cotton and artificial silk, France, c.1931**

A mosaic abstract pattern with repeating red and yellow angular shapes ornaments this woven furnishing fabric. The speckled effect on each shape was introduced in the weave.

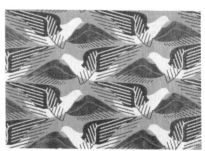

**Rayon and cotton, England, 1939**

The repeating tessellated pattern on 'Avis', a furnishing fabric designed by Marion Dorn, features white dove motifs in flight, with interlacing dark blue and light green wings. The thin blue and white lines on the wings reinforce the idea of motion.

**Silk, France, c.1931**

A pattern called 'Variations', by Robert Bonfils, typifies the Art Deco style after the late 1920s through its use of abstract motifs and muted colours. They are combined with geometric shapes to make clever reference to the imagery of moving machine parts.

# Navajo

### 19th–20th Century

Navajo blankets and rugs are instantly recognisable in style and good examples are highly sought after by collectors. Although these objects have been made in Arizona and New Mexico since the 1700s, the classic period only developed from the 1850s onwards. Since then a large number of patterns have been produced. Specific pieces can often be identified with one of the 13 weaving regions on the Navajo Reservation that in turn give their name to a style. Although Navajo culture is steeped in symbolism, their rugs often do not reflect any sacred significance or imagery.

### Wool, Navajo, c.1863–8

Strong, boldly drawn geometric images dominate this blanket in a symmetrical pattern of diamonds, and solid and broken lines, fringed with half-diamonds at the edges. These motifs seem to have been introduced in the mid 19th century, the so-called transitional period.

**Wool, Navajo, c.1890–5**

A blanket that uses a simple cross motif in differing ways. It has been suggested that the cross is associated with missionary symbolism, but in this piece it is more likely to refer to traditional Navajo imagery, developed before contact with Christianity.

**Wool, Navajo, c.1930s**

With an energetic design based on a range of variously scaled diamond shapes, this woollen rug works well in repeat. The pattern is clearly defined along its vertical axis, but is also broken up by the smaller applied lozenges within the main diamonds.

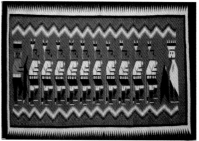

**Wool, detail, Navajo, date unknown**

Part of a woven blanket showing the simple yet subtle mix of geometric combinations these pieces are known for. The zigzag lines could represent lightning: in Navajo folklore the god of lightning carried bolts that were used as ladders, and the zigzags here may be a rare symbolic reference.

**Wool, Navajo, c.1940s**

An unusual motif of a line of abstracted uniformed figures on patrol, with a leader wearing a Navajo blanket, ornaments this woollen rug. The main pictorial image is bordered by a traditional wavy-line motif and an interesting comb effect at the top and bottom.

# Pre-Columbian

### Ancient to Modern

The indigenous peoples of South America have left a rich legacy of pattern-making both on textiles and other artefacts. The role of myths and symbols is deeply rooted in their pattern-making traditions, and completed pieces may have great spiritual importance. Snakes, falling figures, warriors and many versions of geometric designs work in several different countries across Central and South America, although each has its own traditions.

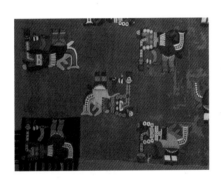

**Wool, Peru, c.200BC–AD200**
A hybrid anthropomorphic figure of a demon or god from an ancient pantheon is the main motif on this mantle. The highly formalised figure has a snake in its mouth and a fish-like tail that add to the powerful impression it makes.

**Feathers, Peru, c.900–1476**
This piece of status clothing – a panel from a cape – is made from the colourful feathers of the macaw parrot and is decorated with a wave motif that resembles the Vitruvian scroll of ancient Rome, suggesting that the spiral scroll is a universal motif.

**Cotton, Peru, c.1100–1500**
Chimu textiles from the northern coast of Peru often feature stylised motifs and geometric figures that repeat themselves in friezes. This example shows a human figure with a large crescent headdress, accompanied by a cat, revered in Chimu culture as the 'bringer of food'.

**Wool, Peru, 14th century**
This tapestry woven panel is composed of alternating squares featuring large fish and birds eating fish. The combination of naïve imagery with a sophisticated pattern arrangement makes it a virtuoso example of the skills of the indigenous peoples of South America.

**Dyes on paper, France, 1960s**
An exotic pattern that takes classic pre-Columbian imagery for its inspiration, and transfers it to a dress fabric. The motifs are composed in blocks of geometric frames, which repeat along the material but in different colour variations, stressing the complexity of the final effect.

# Festival of Britain

## 20th Century

An influential episode in pattern-making took place in the early 1950s when the 1951 Festival of Britain showcased the work of the Festival Pattern Group, which linked designers and scientists. The scientists were analysing the atomic structures of materials by taking X-rays of their crystalline structures and the patterns that resulted from the process were adapted to textile design by well-known designers. They produced a range of abstract furnishing fabrics based on the intricate patterns of crystal structures, thus creating some of the most memorable patterns linked to the 'Contemporary' 1950s style.

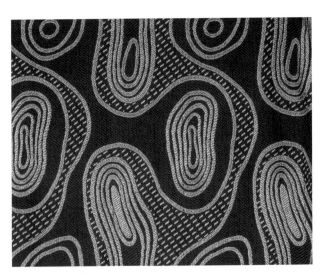

**Wool, cotton and rayon, England, 1951**
'Surrey', a furnishing fabric designed by Marianne Straub, uses the crystal structure of the mineral afwillite and transforms it into a modern, flowing pattern.

**Linen, England, 1951**

One of the best-known examples of the 'Contemporary' style of the 1950s, this design by Lucienne Day is called 'Calyx' in reference to the fruiting body of a flower. The design is clearly inspired by the work of artists such as Paul Klee and Joan Miró and was initially conceived as a collage.

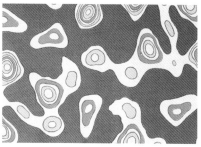

**Rayon, England, 1951**

A screenprinted dress fabric, designed by S.M. Slade, which was inspired by the same mineral as Marianne Straub's 'Surrey' (opposite), but which is named 'Afwillite' directly after it. The pattern was considered particularly appropriate for application to textiles due to its repetitive symmetry.

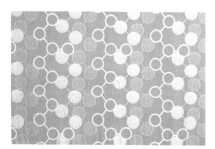

**Cotton, England, 1951**

A geometric pattern referring to the atomic model for nylon is the basis of the Jacquard-weave furnishing fabric, 'Helmsley', designed by Marianne Straub. The linked circles represent different types of atoms.

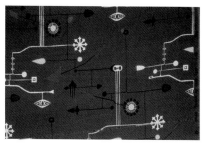

**Cotton, England, 1954**

The mobile or kinetic art of artists such as Alexander Calder provided the inspiration for 'Mobile', a printed furnishing fabric by June Lyon, although it does also seem to be influenced by the work of Joan Miró.

# Psychedelic

**20th Century**

Psychedelic design refers to the counter-cultural art movement of the 1960s in which altered states of awareness were reflected in the products of art and design of the time. These included album covers and graphics, as well as textiles, ceramics and any other objects that could be ornamented by surface pattern. The designs were distinguished by a kaleidoscopic palette of clashing and sometimes outrageous colours, either in strict repeats or swirling, looser patterns. Although the imagery was often abstract, some designs reflected an interest in revolution and socio-political issues.

**Dyes on paper, France, c.1960s**
Patterns of the 1960s were particularly associated with the real or imaginary effects of psychedelic experiences. These included abstract and uncoordinated designs, and garish, jarring colours used in juxtaposition, as in this example.

**Cotton, England, 1964**
Designed by Shirley Craven for Hull Traders Ltd. and entitled 'Division', this screenprinted furnishing fabric looks like a collage or a painting on a large scale. The effect of the contrasting colours and abstract shapes places it firmly in the 1960s.

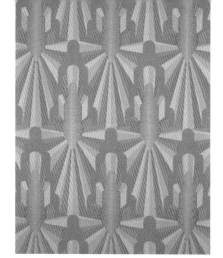

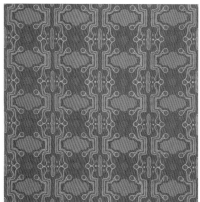

**Cotton, England, 1968**
This furnishing fabric is from a range called 'Stereoscopic,' which featured patterns inspired by charts used by opticians testing for colour-blindness. The ziggurat motif and the jazzy colours hark back to the influences of Art Deco.

**Cotton, Britain, 1969**
The end of the 1960s witnessed an Art Deco revival in design. In this printed furnishing fabric entitled 'Volution', and designed by Peter Hall for Heal Fabrics, the fan

shapes in the centre of the design and the large volutes emulate 1930s architectural ornamentation.

**Cotton, England, 1968**
'Circuit', a screenprinted furnishing fabric, was designed by Eddie Squires for Warner & Sons. The pattern was probably inspired by the electronic circuits used in contemporary technology and is a good example of how a novel idea can be turned into a vivid but relatively conventional repeat.

# Contemporary

### 21st Century

The use of abstract patterning has continued very successfully into the 21st century, and shows all the signs of the inventive pattern-maker. Use has been made of abstracted or stylised natural images, simple but elegant geometry, and humorous and even unexpected imagery – all combined with a lively colour palette. The pattern range is enormous, but is still frequently generated by traditional motifs and styles, often with a post-modern twist. Interest in fashion and interiors has never been greater, so the demand for exciting and novel patterns continues. This selection demonstrates the variety of patterns being developed through inspired responses to decorative stimuli.

**Proof cotton, England, 2006**
This pattern, here applied to a waterproofed fabric shopping bag, but which has been produced in many variations, was designed by Orla Kiely. The multi-stemmed leaves, in the most basic shapes, are an extreme abstraction. Combined with a dynamic colour palette, this pattern reflects the designer's retro sources, from the 1960s and 1970s.

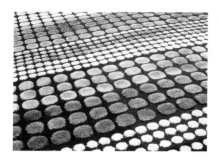

### Rug, England, 2008

A hand-crafted piece in wool, silk and banana-fibre rug, designed by Margo Selby. Her individual use of colour and the strong geometric pattern, based on a single circular bead shape, create a vivid artwork for the floor.

### Silk, England, 2008

A hand-printed dupion textile patterned with an unusual treatment of a briar plant, designed by Clarissa Hulse. The abstracted plant image flows freely across the fabric and is enhanced by the sumptuous selection of colours.

### Linen, England, 2008

Neisha Crosland has designed this elegant print entitled 'Gypsy'. Based around a stylised fern leaf, which appears to unfurl as you watch, it shows how imagery from nature can still be used in original ways to create a pattern that is fresh and visually exciting.

### Lace, Scotland, 2008

A new twist on traditional cotton lace has these superb and realistic thistles, the national emblem of Scotland, depicted very boldly and realistically in a vertical repeat. The natural colours have been abstracted to black and white, to great effect.

# Introduction

The application of realistic object imagery to pattern is one of the best known types of decoration. Object patterns differ from conversational patterns in that they usually depict individual items as opposed to scenes or pictures. Patterns that include objects may render them literally or abstract them to some degree to vary the effect. They range from small repeats of common objects such as flowerpots and screws to large and complicated architectural compositions: equally they may be active images of things in use or passive simple repeats of a single object.

**Cotton, England, c.1805**
From about 1800 to 1840 there was a fashion for chintz designs that depicted complete or broken classical columns, often festooned with flowers, ribbons, birds or baskets of fruit. These designs were particularly fashionable in the United States.

**Cotton, detail, Japan, 19th century**
Taken from a large hanging with silk embroidery, measuring 284 x 278cm (112 x 110in), this piece is one of many that Japanese embroiderers produced for the Western market. It is ornamented with a pattern of scattered fans, each of which has a separate pictorial design.

**Cotton, England, c.1937**

Entitled 'Surfers', this dress fabric has a very dynamic composition showing women surfing on air-beds. The notion of healthy, outdoor living was popular in the 1930s, and with their fashionable bathing suits in contrasting shades of red, white and navy, these figures conform to the current trend.

**Rayon, France, c.1940s**

A delightfully whimsical pattern of cheerfully painted crockery on shelves, designed to be used as a dress fabric. Taking these objects from their everyday context and putting them into a repeat pattern created a bright, accessible pattern for a fashionable material.

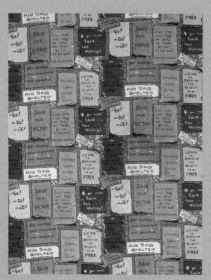

**Rayon, Britain, mid 20th century**

Jacqmar Ltd was noted for its patriotic scarves illustrating aspects of wartime Britain, the first of which was issued in 1941. This headscarf, entitled 'London Wall', features the wartime propaganda slogans that would have been found on walls and hoardings around the capital.

# Calligraphy & Lettering

### 14th–20th Century

Calligraphy (literally 'beautiful writing'), has long been an art form in its own right. Motifs of letters and lettering have been widely used, especially in Islamic ornament and across much of the Far East, but examples occur worldwide. In particular, religious texts are often inserted into Muslim textiles as an act of piety – Arabic script in which the Koran is written lends itself extremely well to incorporation into more complex patterns. In China, calligraphy on paper is considered an art form, so its transference to textiles is not surprising, especially as single symbols can be read for their meanings as well as used ornamentally.

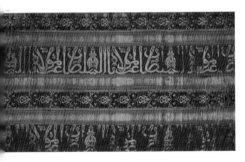

**Silk, Spain, late 14th century**
A panel of Hispano-Moresque woven lampas with alternating bands of calligraphy and floral motifs. The phrase 'Glory to our lord the sultan' has been repeated within the widest band in the design, creating the impression of a long frieze of calligraphy.

**Carpet, detail, Persia, mid 16th century**
On one end of the famous Ardabil Carpet is a small panel of calligraphy, showing the date of completion as the year 946 in the Muslim calendar, equivalent to 1539–40. Much like an artist signing a painting, it also includes the name of the man in charge of the carpet's production, Maqsud Kashani.

## Cotton, France, 1886

In this printed dress fabric, letters have been stylised to the point at which they are no longer immediately readable, and have been placed in a way that makes them seem to tumble down the cloth. Smaller scroll shapes, like floating leaves, add to the lively impression.

## Silk, China, late 19th century

Red is hugely significant in China as a life-giving colour, so the selection of crimson for this celebration banner is not surprising. The Chinese calligraphic character for 'Long Life' is embroidered in gold work in the centre, surrounded by the names of those who donated to its making.

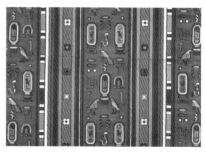

## Cotton, England, early 20th century

The regular pattern of bands of vertical lines overlaid with Egyptian motifs and with hieroglyphic writing on this roller-printed furnishing fabric reflects the massive popular interest in ancient Egypt following the discovery of Tutankhamun's tomb in 1922.

# Domestic

### 19th–20th Century

While everyday objects have been an inspiration for artists since at least the end of the 19th century, they are less universally used on textiles. Nevertheless, various domestic items have made their way over to fabric patterns. There is an air of light-hearted amusement in the resulting material, which sees common – even mundane – items isolated from their context and then included in a fabric repeat. Some objects remain immediately recognisable, whilst others are fairly abstract in their representation.

**Silk, Japan, 19th century**

A *fukusa* or gift cover, embroidered and painted with three gold fans. Fans were traditionally believed to act as a screen against evil in Japan. In a witty touch, the fans, themselves everyday objects, are used to frame others – a rake and a broom – which might be seen as even more ordinary.

**Cotton, France, 1887**

A roller-printed dress fabric using motifs of playing cards and dice underlines the clamour for novelty that textile designers are required to meet, and the range of props that they must use in creating ever-fresh patterns.

**Silk, USA, 1927**

The photographer Edward Steichen designed this unusual abstracted pattern called 'Mothballs and Sugar Cubes'. Ultimately used on a dress fabric, the design is taken from a photograph of the two subjects, lit from different angles, to create a formalised motif of black, grey and white.

**Cotton, Britain, 1946**

Luggage and beach umbrellas set the scene on a screenprinted dress fabric with a light-hearted holiday motif. Although the suitcases and bags are rendered in some detail, the drop repeat is extremely simple and straightforward.

**Synthetic fibres, Japan, 1978**

A small piece of printed textile found in a sample book features a pattern of partially open bamboo umbrellas (*wagasa*), in a regular, rhythmic repeat. The use of such a familiar object in such an ordered way gives the design a pleasing homeliness.

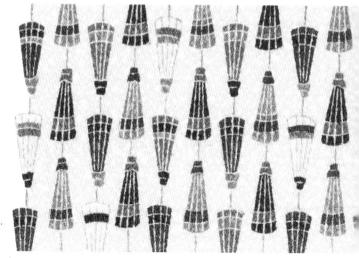

# Machines & Tools

### 19th–20th Century

Although it might seem that tools and machinery make rather a workmanlike and inappropriate basis for textile patterns, they have been used successfully in many applications. The selection here suggests the sheer variety in this category, from images of heavy-duty architectural components to delicate French patterns representing the small parts of watches and clocks. Many of them could be construed as abstract because the components are reduced to the point at which they become simply small repeats, but recognising the objects is part of the fun.

**Cotton, France, c.1880**
That nothing is too eccentric to be used by the pattern maker is illustrated by this roller-printed novelty dress fabric, which not only features a neatly built wall with regular window embrasures, but also shows a regular repeat – highlighted in red – of the S-shaped iron anchor plates that hold the wall safely.

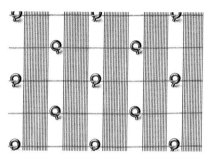

**Cotton, France, 1888**

A roller-printed design with a pattern comprising panels of vertical stripes with screw-eyes rendered very accurately in three dimensions, with a red thread running through them. The optical illusion is quite effective, as is the resultant grid effect.

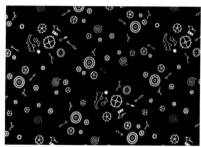

**(Unknown), France, 1937**

Recognisable watch parts are seemingly scattered at random across the fabric in this delicate pattern. The abstract shapes created by the disassociation of the different parts of the watch appear to be floating in space in a rather surreal manner.

**(Unknown), France, 1937**

This simple pattern featuring irregular repeats of pairs of scissors is enlivened by the subtle reflection of the oversized shadows behind each pair. There is an understated humour in using an image of the dressmaker's scissors that will eventually be cutting the fabric into a dress.

**(Unknown), France, 1938**

The use of quantities of overlaid cogs on this printed fabric reflects the contemporary interest in speed and motion that was a hallmark of the Art Deco period which, by this comparatively late period, was supplying the inspiration for quite ordinary prints, as well as for more luxurious ones.

# Toys

### 19th–20th Century

The range of toy imagery used by the pattern designer has varied down the ages as the taste in playthings changes. Like other objects, toys may be stylised or accurate representations, but in most cases form and colour are the key elements. Whichever way they are planned, in elegant repeats or as an apparently random tumbling, the effect of these fabrics is invariably playful and attractive. An ironic tension is created when an object we associate with childhood and simplicity is used to create an adult, sophisticated fabric.

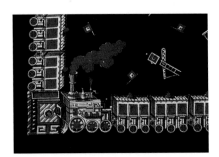

**Wool challis, detail, France, 1887**
Although this pattern is found on a woman's scarf, the trains that run around the border are clearly inspired by a child's toy set. The middle of the scarf is scattered with a vivid arrangement of flags and signals associated with the railway, and the colour contrasts of the whole piece are strong and striking.

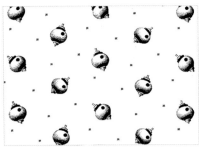

**Cotton, France, 1888**
An early roller-printed fabric, which nonetheless has a modern feel about it. What appears to be a neat and quite sophisticated repeat repays closer attention: regular red dots are mingled with a simple, shaded rendering of a child's spinning top, set at different angles across the fabric.

## Design for fabric, France, 1930s

A number of toys and games of the period feature on this material, intended for making up into children's wear. Tumbling down the fabric, the vividly coloured toys fall over and through a background made up of letters of the alphabet.

## Rayon, England, 1936

A printed crêpe material entitled 'Fun & Games' showing images that evoke all the fun of the fair, with flags and lanterns, bunting and a miniature rifle range. The effect is an energetic and enjoyable pattern.

## Cotton, Finland, 2008

Finnish company Marimekko's 'Pikku Bo Boo' is used on a range of children's products, including this duvet cover. Designed by Katsuji Wakisaka, it features simplified large-scale trucks, buses and cars in bright, bold colours reminiscent of nursery toys.

# Gardens

### 17th–20th Century

The deep-seated affection that many people have for flowers and plants clearly extends to gardens and their representation. This selection shows a range of gardening imagery from small motifs to grand formal gardens. In a symbolic sense, and particularly in Middle Eastern cultures, the garden represents earthly paradise at the centre of the cosmos and an image of the heavenly paradise to come. Offering natural motifs and both formal and informal arrangements, gardens are an ideal inspiration for pattern-making.

**Wool, England c.1600–20**
A hand-knotted pile panel depicting different types of flowers, each one contained within its own architectural arch. The marigolds, carnations, grape-vine, pansies, roses and strawberry plants were commonly found in English gardens of the 17th century, and the rigid layout is reminiscent of Tudor knot gardens.

**Linen, England, c.1710–20**

This canvas hanging, embroidered with silk and wool, with some details in appliqué, depicts scenes from Stoke Edith, Herefordshire, where formal gardens were laid out in the late 17th-century Anglo-Dutch style. The large scale and the fine quality of the piece suggests it was professionally worked.

**Linen, Turkey, 19th century**

Embroidered with silk and metal thread, this towel or napkin features a formal repeating motif of alternating lemon trees and pink fruit trees planted in blue and gilt pots. Miniature triangular trees laden with golden fruit separate the larger motifs.

**Cotton and satin, England, c.1923**

A furnishing fabric with an irregular pattern of garden imagery, showing various exotic plants and fruit trees in planters, surrounded by blue trellises and light orange walkways. The unnatural colour scheme is typically Art Deco.

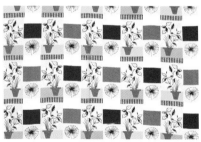

**Rayon, England, 1954**

This roller-printed furnishing fabric features a chequered background and superimposed motif typical of the mid 1950s. The effect is clean, light-hearted and, in contrast with the often dark or more sophisticated palette of the previous decade, looks fresh and modern.

# Architecture

### 16th–20th Century

Whether by means of literal representations of buildings, or of imaginary, stylised or abstract versions, architecture and its components can make interesting designs for textiles. In pattern-making terms, architectural elements can be used as simple repeats of the same patterns, as individual 'pictures' or as multiple representations of architectural scenes used in a more random way. The range of possibilities is enormous and these pages show just a few examples.

**Silk and linen, Italy, 16th century**
A woven napkin with a banded decoration of lions, floral motifs, vases and – most strikingly – architectural motifs of elaborate small castles or pavilions. Although this item was used as a napkin, such textiles were also used to cover the principal place setting of a table.

**Throne cover, detail, India, 18th century**
A fine embroidered piece that would have been used as a throne cover or *takhtposh*, featuring multi-coloured metal threads in its workings. This detail of the centre panel shows a landscape with fine buildings rendered in some detail and traversed by a band depicting ships and birds on water.

**Cotton, Ottoman Empire, 19th century**
The repeating pattern on the border of this towel is typical of Ottoman designs for similar household objects. This one has tall buildings alternating with trees and gardens.

**Silk, detail, Japan, 19th century**
Part of a gift cover, or *fukusa*, with silk embroidery. The scene of an island castle and a bridge are finely rendered in gold embroidery, which looks particularly striking against the rich, blue ground.

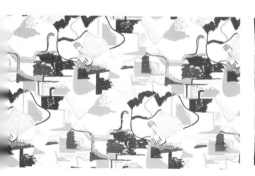

**Linen, France, c.1920s**
An Art Deco design by architect and designer Pierre Chareau. The block-printed motifs in grey, muted brown and yellow create an almost surreal landscape, in which the viewer sees buildings and chimneys. The repeats draw the eye diagonally across the field.

**Cotton, France, c.1925–30**
The pattern on this woven plush upholstery fabric appears abstract at first glance, but a second look seems to reveal a bird's eye view of a modern housing estate, in which all the units are repeated both on the ground and in the pattern.

# Architecture

**Viscose, England, 1936**

Printed with roundels of tourist sights of London, this cloth was made to mark a coronation that never happened – that of Edward VIII in 1936. This is a pattern that would readily be used on a variety of souvenir goods for London visitors and it is timeless in its appeal.

**Cotton, Britain, c.1950–4**

A screenprinted dress fabric designed by the London-based Ascher Studio, which depicts a Mediterranean harbour scene, complete with small boats used as fillers in the plain blue bands that link the rows of buildings. The colours reflect the bright palette of Greece or Italy, but the repeat is simple and standard.

**Cotton, England, 1952**

A screenprinted furnishing fabric designed by Mary Oliver. Like the piece on the left, the repeating pattern depicts an Italian seaside village, complete with boats in harbour. Although the design is pretty and straightforward, the exotic landscape it suggests would have been out of reach for most Britons in the 1950s.

**Cotton, England, 1994**

Entitled 'Forum of Frescoes', this screenprint was designed and manufactured by Timney Fowler Ltd. A good example of the witty use of traditional art and architectural elements juxtaposed with and overlaid by a repeat pattern that is vibrant in both composition and colouring.

# Air & Space Travel

### 20th Century

From glamorous innovation in the 1920s and 30s to commonplace mode of transport by the end of the 20th century, air travel has been celebrated by designers in a wide range of fabrics, but still has a sense of excitement about it. A darker side of air power is the use of aircraft in war, and this has not been ignored by pattern-makers either. Alongside flight and aircraft imagery are patterns associated with space travel. Particularly in the 1960s and 70s textile designers picked up on the fascination for space exploration and produced both fanciful and realistic designs, many suitable for use in children's rooms.

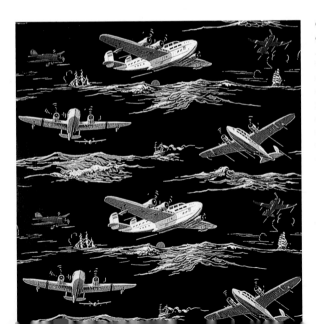

**Cotton, USA, c.1930s–40s**
A striking pattern with a transport theme, and a great sense of movement. The majestic flying boat and its small red companion appear to dwarf both the steam and sailing ships.

**Linen and rayon, England, 1938**

'Aircraft', a screenprinted furnishing fabric designed by Marion Dorn. The slightly menacing shapes of showy birds/aeroplanes draw on ancient imperial imagery of eagles. This fabric was used for upholstery in the lounge of the ocean liner *Orcades*.

**Cotton, England, 1941**

Loaded with patriotic messages, 'Victory V' is characteristic of the fabrics that were produced – mainly for apparel – during the Second World War. The border of three dots and a dash represents the Morse code for 'victory'.

**Cotton, England, 1969**

A multi-coloured print, designed by Sue Palmer for Warner & Sons, entitled 'Space Walk'. The pattern, which is a mirror repeat, picks up on the contemporary interest and excitement generated by the novelty of space travel.

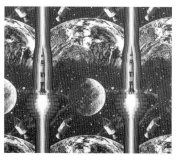

**Cotton, England, 1970**

'Lunar Rocket', a screenprinted furnishing fabric, commemorates the moon landing in 1969. The straightforward repeat of Earth and moon flanked by firing rockets is now recognised as a cult classic in design terms, although it was not commercially successful at the time.

# Introduction

Stripes using straight lines, either in vertical or horizontal arrangements, or crossed at various angles in a grid form, are one of the most basic pattern arrangements. This selection looks at basic stripes and checks along with more complex basketweaves, tartans, plaids and other grid effects. The use of grids as a framework for patterning is sometimes driven by the craft of weaving – in which checks can be naturally produced – and sometimes by the demands of the pattern-maker.

**Cotton, France, c.1810–20**
A novelty repeat pattern for a dress fabric, with three distinct elements: a set of joined vertical wavy lines, another set of thin wavy lines between them, and stylised plant forms overlaid on the narrower stripes. There is an element of optical illusion to this pattern, which seems to move slightly as the eye looks at it, and then away.

### Wool, Tunisia, c.1850

Originally displayed in the Great Exhibition at Crystal Palace in 1851. This woven blanket features a set of independent stripes, which have various decorative panels and diamond-shaped motifs inserted within them. They are separated by plain areas of ground, bisected by a single, simple stripe.

### Cotton, USA, 1860s

The use of basket or latticework to create a grid-like structure is a key textile motif. This printed example takes the idea and creates the illusion of a webbed or interlocked surface with small spaces revealed between the straps.

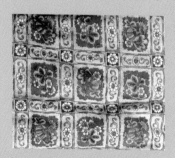

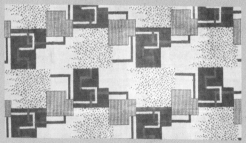

### Cotton, Japan, 19th century

This detail of a bedding cover known as a *yogi* is made from *sarasa*, a type of cloth related to Indian and Southeast Asian block-printed and wax-resist textiles imported into Japan. The simple grid is enlivened by the applied decoration.

### Cotton, France, c.1925

A plush furnishing fabric with an interesting network pattern, formed from three major rectangles of various shapes and finishes, linked together by lines to create a repeating structure. The criss-cross nature of the pattern serves to emphasise the overall grid.

# Simple Stripes

### 19th–21st Century

Although they are amongst the simplest of patterns, and are often relegated to the sidelines of pattern-making, stripes can be interesting. In some terminology, striped textiles refer to any pattern that has motifs lined up vertically; in other cases, stripes refer to regular (usually vertical) bands of alternating colours. Stripes can be produced in any width (within reason) and in any suitable colour combination. They remain one of the most popular options in furnishing and fashion patterns.

**Cotton, West Africa, 19th century**

An embroidered robe in the pattern style of 'strip cloth' that is widely used throughout much of West Africa. On this piece, from Liberia, the combination of diamond shapes on stripes is simple but effective, and the overall vertical stripes emphasise the height of the wearer.

**Silk, detail, Eastern Turkestan, late 19th or early 20th century**

This detail of the button enclosure of a robe shows magenta damask ornamented with ornate gold double paisley motifs, all mounted on a multi-coloured striped background. The vivid colours of the stripes dominate the pattern.

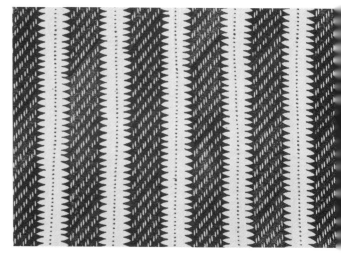

## Linen, England, 1930s

Called 'Pointed Pip', this block-print shows the influence of lino-block printing, developed by Phyllis Barron and Dorothy Larcher in the 1920s and 30s. The pointed edges on the stripes make the pattern appear to 'move' slightly when viewed.

## Cotton, England, 1954

Designed by the 'outsider artist' Scottie Wilson, who was well known for his simple botanical images, this pattern is appropriately known as 'Scottie Stripe', and features a screenprinted design of stylised birds on water and rocks.

## Polyester, linen, silk and lurex, England, 2008

Ticking is normally associated with black and white utilitarian stripes for mattresses. This luxury version with metallic threads and silk plays with the perception of a plain, hardworking textile, serving it up in an unrecognisably lavish form.

# Combinations

### 19th–20th Century

Striped patterns are often associated with quite humble and hardworking textiles, such as mattress ticking and tea towels. Stripes are, however, the basis for many other patterns, including chevrons, ginghams and plaids and some striped materials can be very sophisticated, especially if woven with other detail or worked in subtle yarn colours. Striped patterns often appear to their best advantage when used on a relatively flat surface, such as walls, bedspreads or Roman blinds.

**Silk, India, late 19th century**
This cloth from Benares in Uttar Pradesh is known as *charkhana sangi*, a reference to its light and subtle check. The predominant stripes are softened by the light horizontal cross effects.

**Silk and cotton, Persia, c.1876**
An elaborate woven piece with a range of different stripes: red and white with red and blue floral motifs, and further thin strips of black and yellow. The strong horizontal emphasis reflects the weaving process well.

**Cotton, England, 1921**
This roller-printed Art Deco furnishing fabric features a regular pattern of mixed geometric shapes, including strong vertical lines, squares and circles, combined with vertical red and white hatched rectangles on a pale-blue background.

**Linen, Sweden, 1956**
A simple screenprinted furnishing fabric with a vertical pattern reminiscent of bamboo, designed by Astrid Sampe for the Swedish retailer Nordiska Kompaniet. It is a fine example of a typically simple but elegant Swedish design.

**Cotton, England, 1960**
'Intermission', a furnishing fabric designed by Barbara Brown for Heal Fabrics. This pattern, an updated take on stripes, has heavy, dark vertical stripes overlaid with circles of various sizes. The colour scheme places this textile firmly in the 1960s.

# Checks

### 19th Century

Checks are patterns consisting of crossed horizontal and vertical bands in two or more colours, produced by weaving or printing. The grid that is used to create a check pattern usually has uniform vertical and horizontal stripes, whereas a plaid often has stripes of various widths. Japanese designers have a tradition of creating interesting check patterns since the 18th century. Some check patterns have become so established that they have their own names, such as the Scottish District check, which was sometimes made with contrasting overplaids, and Buffalo check, which has blocks of two or three contrasting colours.

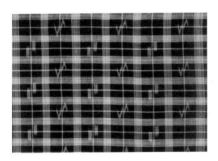

**Cotton, Japan, 19th century**
This Japanese cotton cloth, woven with selectively pre-dyed yarns (*kasuri*) in a combination of stripes and checks bears some resemblance to a Scottish tartan. The delicate overlaid tick shapes and double rectangles add subtle detailing.

**Cotton, fragment, Japan, 19th century**
A striped plain-weave fabric from the Tamba district of Japan. This textile fragment, in pale brown with black, white and blue stripes, is similar in type to some fabrics created for utilitarian uses in the West. The narrow repeated horizontal bands soften the vertical emphasis.

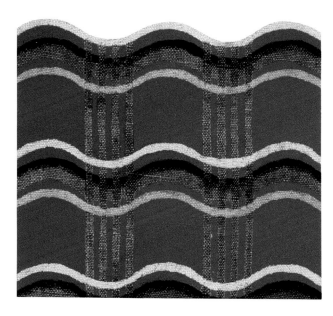

**Cotton, France, c.1810–20**
Drawing inspiration from the traditional costumes of Provence, which are characterised by their bright colour palette and striped patterns, this dress fabric has a gentle check effect, formed by straight verticals crossed by broad, wavy horizontal bands.

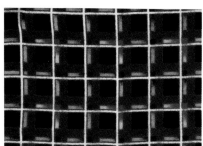

**Wool, France, c.1850**
A challis dress fabric printed with a check pattern that is intended to replicate the look of woven cloth. The shapes in the top corners of each main square give the motif a slightly three-dimensional effect.

**Cotton and silk, Baluchistan/ Pakistan, 1872**
A woven bed cover with strong vertical stripes is made more interesting by the introduction of lighter horizontal lines resulting in a gentle check. The intersection of each square is highlighted by a small motif consisting of a square within a circle.

# Basketweave & Lattice

### 19th–20th Century

The distinctions between basketweave and lattice patterns can be rather blurred, as both are usually made up as a geometric grid of rows crossing under and over one another. The basket-weaving tradition is ancient and clearly has links with the weaving process. In textile patterns, a basket or lattice design may or may not attempt a *trompe l'oeil* effect in which the bands are shown 'woven' together, but usually has some features that make it a little more elaborate than simply a set of crossed lines.

**Silk, India, mid 19th century**
Embroidered with coloured beads, with a red and yellow check border, and red and black flowers, this square mat, made in Darjeeling in Bengal, is asymmetrical in its patterning. Short lines criss-crossing the piece give the impression of woven pattern.

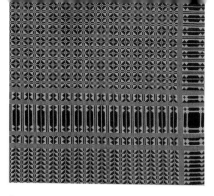

### Cotton, India, mid 19th century

A beautiful and hard-wearing geometrically patterned textile called a *khes*, of a type made in several parts of the Punjab. The main field is filled with tiny detailed patterns, while the border is made with a bolder pattern featuring deep vertical stripes.

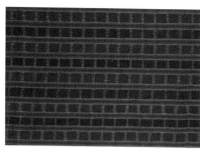

### Silk, India, 1855

Sometimes the distinctions between grids, stripes, basketweave and lattice patterns are quite difficult to determine. In this ikat fabric from Tamil Nadu, there is a clear vertical emphasis, but the grid effect of the crossing parts of the pattern place it firmly in the category of a lattice.

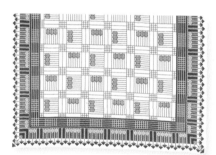

### (Unknown), Austria, 1906

The pattern for this woven tablecloth was designed by Joseph Hoffman for the Wiener Werkstätte in Vienna. The group aimed to produce well-designed products for a select market. Strict geometry is playfully lifted by the angled pointed arrows in the border.

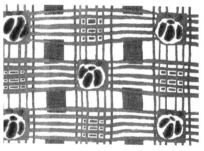

### Cotton, England, 1920s

A furnishing fabric of roller-printed cretonne, on a light grey background with bold vertical, broken black bands and an overlapping, regular pattern of horizontal and vertical lines in blue. The lines are broken by a repeating abstract cerise apple motif, encased in a blue square shape.

# Tartan

### 19th–20th Century

Tartan is a particular pattern made up of crossing horizontal and vertical bands in a range of colours. Originally, all tartans were woven, but tartan patterns are now found in prints, too. Scotland has a particular association with tartan, with different weaves each being associated with a different clan and playing an integral part in clan culture. When a tartan is woven, the weaving process forms visible diagonal lines where different colours cross, giving the appearance of new colours emerging from the existing threads. Tartan patterns repeat vertically and horizontally in a particular sequence of squares and lines called a sett.

**Silk, Scotland, c.1850**

A tartan sash dress ornament in red, blue, yellow and white, and tied at the top with a bow, demonstrates one of the more fashionable applications of tartan for women's dress. The colours in this example are traditional, and the pattern has been cut to take full advantage of the tartan's stripes.

**Wool, England, detail, 1840–60**

A portion of a heavily ornamented cream woven cashmere cape trimmed with tartan ribbon, black lace and a red, blue and green fringe. The photograph shows the hem, with a section of tartan ribbon, next to black fine lace that features a floral or feather pattern.

**Silk, Scotland, c.1850**
The tartan pattern works well on this waistcoat, which was once the centrepiece of a Victorian gentleman's outfit. Made from woven velvet, it features blocks of colour repeated vertically and horizontally to create a sett. While patterns at this date often copied genuine tartans, others were fanciful designs.

**Silk, England, c.1850**
This tartan chatelaine bag, with thistle embroidery, would have been worn suspended from the belt of a crinoline skirt, fixed by a cord or chain. Such accessories would often be matched to dress fabric so that they could be the finishing touches to a particular outfit.

**Wool, England, c.1851**
This machine-knit sock manufactured by the firm of I. & R. Morley Ltd, London, reflects the contemporary taste for all things Scottish that took hold of England in the mid 19th century. Queen Victoria, herself a great enthusiast, set the trend by using tartan in her dress and decoration.

# Tartan

### 19th–20th Century

Although tartans have a long and sometimes romanticised history, it appears that it was not until the mid 1800s that specific tartans became associated with particular Scottish clans or families. In any event, the taste for tartan spread rapidly in England and English-speaking countries as Queen Victoria embraced the traditions of Scotland and Scottishness. Tartan is also known as plaid, although plaid is actually a generic term for chequered cloth.

### Silk, France, c.1925

Designed by Paul Poiret, this stylish tartan dress in unusual colours seems to epitomise the taste for bizarre or uncommon materials and effects that was one part of the Art Deco style.

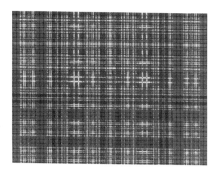

**Design for fabric, Scotland, c.1886**

The 'sett' of a tartan is its colour sequence and arrangement, which is defined by the exact number of threads required for each warp colour-stripe. In weaving tartans, the exact colour numbers and sequence must be maintained in the weft as well as in the warp, to create a balanced plaid.

**Design for fabric, Scotland, c.1886**

A classic tartan of two colours, often called 'Rob Roy' after the eponymous hero – a member of the MacGregor clan – of Sir Walter Scott's popular novel. This pattern existed long before distinct tartans became connected to specific clans.

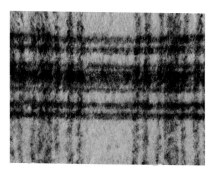

**Cotton, USA, c.1950–90**

This American 'tartan' dress fabric is a sham twice over. Not only is it a printed design that imitates the traditional woven pattern, but it does not have any direct relationship with the 'true' tartan patterns originating from Scotland.

**Mohair, wool and nylon, Britain, c.1957**

An unusual textile sample in which a black check is laid out in a way similar to a tartan 'sett' on a green ground. The effect is intriguing, and a demonstration of how texture can change the nature of even a conventional pattern.

# Grid Frameworks

### Ancient to Modern

The grid is the basic template or framework for any textile design with a repeat pattern, and is fundamental for the pattern-maker planning a repeat. In the past, designs were often worked out on gridded paper so that the particular warp and weft threads of the weaves could be identified, a job that is now done using computer programs. Although the grid is very common in textile pattern, this selection shows how varied the results have been at different times. Elements of other grid types can be seen in some of them, including diaper, trellis, lozenge and even ogee shapes – all of which have the grid as their common denominator.

### Silk, Egypt, c.600–899

A sophisticated pattern combination of rosettes in circles, with stepped borders in pink and white makes this very early panel distinctive. The grid is maintained by clever use of the stepped frame around the circular motifs.

### Silk, Byzantium, c.1200–1399

This panel is woven with a large trellis-type background that features flower heads and lozenges alternately inserted into the framed spaces. The grid itself is fitted with small rosettes following the diaper pattern. The purple dye identifies this as a costly and luxurious piece.

**(Unknown), Greece, 18th century**
It is possible to see squares, diamonds and even stylised circles in the pattern on this curtain fabric, which has been put together with a mixture of weaving and embroidery techniques.

**Linen, England, 18th century**
The skills of the needleworker are evident in the regularity of the panels in this small-scale 'tiled' pattern in coloured wool and silk Florentine stitch on canvas. The floral motifs are set in neat contrast to the geometric diamonds.

**Wool, Canada, c.1860**
The twill-diaper weave produces self-patterned textiles with rectilinear designs, formed by the contrast of the warp and weft faces. The 'table' and 'roses' design of this coverlet creates a grid that is subtly overlaid with floral shapes.

# Plaids & Tweeds

### 19th–20th Century

Plaids are woven or printed patterns comprising warp and weft stripes woven in plain or twill weave that form different colours in square or rectangular patterns. Technically, tartans are a specific form of plaid, and printed plaid patterns are also sometimes categorised as 'gingham shirting' and 'French provincials'. Tweed can be either an apparel or upholstery-weight material made in plain or twill weave and may have a check or herringbone pattern. It is known for its subtle colour effects, which are created by twisting different coloured wools together to create two- or three-ply yarns.

**Cotton, France, c.1880–90**
An example of a roller-printed shirting material sporting a plaid effect. The absolutely geometric grid can be woven or printed in a multitude of colour combinations, making this sort of pattern a popular choice for men's casual shirting.

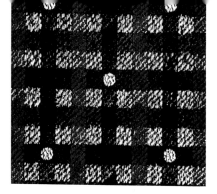

**Gouache on paper, France, c.1900–20**
The benefit of weaving plaids in a grid pattern is that they produce lovely muted colours and textures. This design for an apparel fabric features a dominant black squared grid with blue infill; the whole thing is overlaid with a red stripe, and the occasional white circle lifts the effect.

**Wool, detail, Britain, 1964**
A suit jacket made by Anderson and Sheppard, tailors on London's Savile Row. The jacket is made in the well-known Glen Urquhart check. Although it is often confused with the Prince of Wales check, the genuine Glen Urquhart comes only in black and white – with no colour added.

**Wool, detail, Britain, early 1980s**
A check plaid textile, designed by Vivienne Westwood, and part of a collection called *Buccaneer*, which drew its inspiration from pirate style. The combination of a traditional plaid with outrageous slashed sleeves is typical of Westwood.

**Wool, Britain, 1996**
This detail shows a very English plaid of green and violet check tweed, used in a shooting jacket designed and tailored by Hackett. This cloth, while understated, is both subtle and stylish, with its elegant combination of a gentle check over a plain grey background.

# Modernist

### 20th Century

The designers of the Modern movement, usually seen as dating from 1920 to 1960, sought to reduce or eliminate pattern from their work, as they believed it distracted from the elemental nature of a product or building. In textile terms, this resulted in a renewed interest in patterns made with geometrical forms, and, in woven fabrics, an attention to the potential of the actual weaving process in pattern-making. The attention to geometry often created a direct relationship between the textile patterns produced in this period and the nature of the buildings the fabrics were used in.

**Cotton, Austria, c. 1920–29**
This textile by the Wiener Werkstätte demonstrates Modernism's characteristic grid effects, which provide an ordering structure for the pattern. The design is a complex arrangement of squares or planes within the larger grid, and reflects the Modernist rejection of naturalism.

**Cotton, France, c.1920s–30s**
That the grid format can act as a basis for a design is demonstrated by this simple all-over pattern. The offset squares are linked together to make the grid, which is then completed with abstracted hat-like shapes that fill in the frames.

**Silk, France, 1928**
A roller-printed dress fabric that demonstrates how pattern can be built up from the simplest forms. Using only a stylised screw-head or a coffee bean shape, the alignment of four horizontal shapes counteracted by eight vertical shapes in repeat is stylishly successful.

**Gouache on paper, France, 1930s**
The geometry of this pattern – a combination of squares, circles and stepped lines give this Art Deco design a definite look of its period. The influence of contemporary fine art is also discernable.

**Linen, Ireland, c.1955**
Entitled 'Flight', and designed by Louis le Brocquy, this furnishing fabric features an abstracted running figure, with clear links both to Matisse's silhouette works and to the African art which formed part of his inspiration. The horizontally striped weave helps to ground the dynamic motif.

# Introduction

Representations of the human figure in textiles can be found in most cultures, even though most Sunni and Shia Muslims believe that, generally speaking, representations of living beings should not be used. Nevertheless, images of humans can be found in all eras of Islamic art. Human figures are often used in textile designs for many purposes, but most commonly, they are used to retell stories. This section looks at human figures in a variety of contexts, including mythological representations and images that concentrate on parts of the body.

**Tapestry, detail, France, mid 15th century**
This long, slim Alsatian tapestry would have hung above a bench, and the whole depicts the work of a year. 'September', shown here, shows rural labourers harrowing and sowing.

**Tapestry, detail, England, early 17th century**
A Mortlake weaving from a set that tells the story of Venus and her lover Mars, imprisoned by her husband Vulcan, who sits in judgment on them. Neptune, god of the sea, and Cupid, god of love, plead on behalf of the lovers in this detail.

### Linen, detail, Greece, 18th century

This cream robe was intended for a male user and has a heavily embroidered design around the sleeves, as shown here. Naïve motifs of men, women, flowers, trees and buildings feature in bright colours that contrast with the cream background. The rim of the fabric is further embellished with gold lace.

### Silk, detail, India, mid 19th century

A typically elaborate sari from Bengal of virtuoso woven silk work, full of fine detail. This detail shows a male ruler on a horse complete with female attendants, umbrella and banner.

### Silk, USA, 1927

Entitled 'Gentlemen Prefer Blondes', this crêpe de Chine dress fabric was designed by Ralph Barton. The overlapping, rather abstract pattern shows a blonde, a group of brunettes, and several men in top hats. The name is taken from the novel by Anita Loos, published in 1925.

# Religious

### 13th–19th Century

Patterns that depict religious activities or relate to particular rituals have been included in previous sections. In this selection the designers have created patterns using people associated with specific religious causes. They may show a stylised and imaginary image of an angel, or they may depict particular moments in certain characters' lives. In many cases, the textiles were designed for use in religious ceremonies or for adorning parts of ecclesiastical buildings. In most cases, the reverence inherent in the choice of pattern gave the maker an opportunity to display his or her finest skills in producing these textiles.

**Silk, England, c.1295–1315**
A detail from a medieval embroidery, depicting the Tree of Jesse with silver-gilt and silver thread, and split-stitch with laid and couched work. The Jesse tree is frequent in ecclesiastical art and shows the genealogy of Jesus Christ as it is described in the Gospel of St Matthew.

**Silk, England, c.1320–40**
Panel from a burse, one of the purse-like pouches used to contain corporals, the linen cloths used in the celebration of Mass. The border around the figures is typically medieval in its use of compass work and the whole is heavily embroidered with silver, silver-gilt and silk threads.

**Silk, detail, China, c.1650–1700**
Part of a densely embroidered silk robe worn by a Taoist priest. The 350 deities shown on the whole robe represent the gods of the Taoist pantheon, including the Three Purities, the Three Celestial Worthies and the Jade Emperor.

**Satin, Greece, early 18th century**
An *epitaphios* is a large cloth icon, which is carried in religious processions. This richly adorned example was used during Eastern Orthodox services at Easter time, hence the imagery of a coffin, Christ's body, a canopy and stars. The burgundy colour of the background is traditional.

**Cotton, England, c.1884**
'The Angel with the Trumpet', a block-printed furnishing fabric designed by Herbert Horne. The angel as a bringer of glad tidings was a popular motif in Victorian art. Horne was associated with the Century Guild, which aimed to raise the profile of the 'lesser arts'.

# Mythological

### Ancient to Modern

The term 'classical mythology' refers specifically to the mythologies of Ancient Greece and Rome. These are bodies of stories originating with the ancient Greeks and concern the pantheon of gods and heroes they established to make sense of their world. They have remained a source of fascination for artists and designers ever since. In textile design we can see a range of interpretations in their use as pattern. In some cases a whole scene will be depicted and easily understood; in other cases the imagery is used symbolically or in abstract form.

**Wool and linen, Egypt, c.300–499**
The imagery on this woven panel, which would have been appliquéd onto a tunic, depicts Hermes with his messenger's wand in his left hand. The purse carried in his right hand is a symbol of commerce, because he was also the god of riches.

**Tapestry, England, c.1595**
The 'Judgement of Paris' hanging, woven in wool and silk. Parts of this Sheldon design were taken from prints from a well-known architectural manual, while the birds and flowers were created in a style often found in the southern Netherlands.

### Cotton, England, 1887

Designed by Walter Crane, the complex pattern on this furnishing fabric represents the continents of the world, including a large Viking ship, a Roman centurion's helmet, and representations of women in the different dress characteristic of South Africa, Australia, India, Britain and Canada.

### Silk, England, 1939

Marion Dorn designed this screenprinted furnishing fabric entitled 'Etruscan Head'. The classical warrior profiles are instantly recognisable. The repeat uses the same shapes and details, but in various colourings, and the two opposing aspects are divided by a simple row of stylised leaves.

### Cotton, England, 1939

A printed furnishing fabric called 'Bacchante' – named after a votary or follower of the Roman god Bacchus – composed of a regular pattern of square motifs featuring the figure of a bacchante, a wine pitcher, a vine with grapes and leaves, and a green plant motif.

# Pastoral

### 16th–20th Century

The human figure depicted in a garden or a natural landscape has variously represented a rural, pastoral or even Arcadian way of life. Gardens are an escape from the everyday and are often depicted as places of wonder, ease and contentment. The textiles that best offer the opportunity to express these ideas in pattern are flat panels, such as tapestries and hangings. Their geographic spread is wide, testifying to the attraction of the pastoral design and its multiple possibilities, from the formal arrangement of symbolic elements to bucolic landscapes more naturalistically rendered.

**Linen, detail, England or France, late 16th century**
An embroidered valance depicting a narrative garden scene. In this section the setting is an ornamental garden with a pair of seated lovers. A woman holding a mirror, possibly intended to represent Prudence, attends them.

**Silk, Persia, 17th–18th century**

Embroidered in coloured silks, this pattern has a vertically repeating pattern of hunters carrying bows and arrows surrounded by fantastical creatures in a wood of flowering trees. The amorphous outlined shapes may be intended to represent small lakes.

**Muslin, India, 19th century**

This *rumal*, a handkerchief or bandanna, is embroidered in silk with simple but recognisable scenes depicting a wedding. The tent for the ceremony is central in the pattern, and the surroundings depict guests, furniture and gifts.

**Tapestry, England, 1863**

Entitled 'The Orchard, the Seasons', this piece, designed by William Morris, is woven in wool, silk and mohair on a cotton warp. Typical of Morris, it features figures in medieval robes, Gothic lettering, and plenty of naturalistic trees and flowers.

# Pastoral

**Wool, detail, Burma, c.1880**
The appliqué design on this hanging or *kalaga*, depicting scenes from the Buddha's former lives, is worked in coloured fabrics, painted and ornamented with sequins. The costumes are in the tradition of Burmese theatre.

**Cotton, Ottoman Empire, 19th century**
An embroidered towel with silk and metal threads depicting a repeating image of stylized and over-scaled trees or bushes with monumental figures placed between them. A building is set into a self-contained scene between the legs of the figure.

**Cotton, Ottoman Empire, mid 19th century**
A landscape rich with buildings, and rows of trees and plants, ornaments this napkin embroidered with silk and metal threads. The offset repeat of the four bands makes the pattern look more complex than it is.

**Cotton, Britain, 1929**

A late design by Arts and Crafts architect C.F.A. Voysey, this printed nursery chintz incorporates one of Voysey's houses in the pattern, which is based on a nursery rhyme. A rat motif was left out of later printings.

**Wool, Burma, c.1880–1890**

A *kalaga* or pictorial hanging partly decorated with an appliqué design ornamented with sequins. The design depicts courtly figures dressed in the style of traditional Burmese theatre that was fashionable in the Mandalay court of the period.

**Cotton, China, mid 20th century**

This polychrome cover in resist-dyed pattern, from the Changle region, tells the story of the Hanlin scholar. Hanlin graduates functioned as the emperor's close advisers, and only the most talented students were allowed to join the Hanlin academy.

# Landscape

### 16th–20th Century

The human figure in a landscape develops the 'garden theme' in a full rural location. The countryside is an idyllic image for many, and is commonly depicted as a peaceful, untroubled world of pastoral beauty to escape to. A variety of textiles have been used to express these ideas in pattern and can often be found in toiles, apparel material and furnishing fabrics. The Arcadian image is frequently reinforced with props such as classical ruins or urns, and sometimes set by scenes of pastoral folk drink and dance. Again, this genre is found all over the world and there is a huge range of designs on the theme.

**Silk, Persia, 16th century**
The interest of the Safavid rulers in plants and gardens is reflected in the themes shown on this dress fabric, which depicts men eating and drinking amongst flowers and leaves, in a courtly, relaxed setting.

**Linen canvas, detail, England or France, c.1570–99**

An embroidered valance illustrating a *fête champêtre* or outdoor entertainment. These were often very elegant, with music and games played outside in the open air. The small boy in the foreground is holding the music scores.

**Cotton, England, 1762**

This plate-printed furnishing fabric depicts figures in a conversational group against a backdrop of classical ruins. The scene reflects the interest in both ancient history and the natural world at this time. The girl is focusing on the man as her cattle stray – the moral is the dangers of distraction.

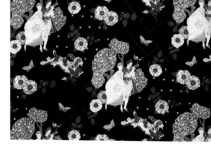

**Linen and cotton, England, 1769**

The repeat on this furnishing fabric, printed from both engraved copper plates and woodblocks, features a figure leaning on a pedestal bearing an urn in a rural landscape. It shares motifs with many figurative paintings of the late 18th century.

**Cotton, England, c.1925**

A roller-printed dress fabric sporting a delightfully ethereal repeating pattern of a couple by a tree, surrounded by a dog running, butterflies, flowers and small white star shapes. The black ground provides a perfect contrast to the design.

# Roundels

### Ancient to Modern

Designs that depict figures within circles may simply be using the loop as a framing device, but often, too, there is a symbolic link with the circle itself, which may be seen either as representing the totality of the human experience or as an image of protection that embraces all within it. The patterns here, from a wide geographic and time span, indicate the importance of circles to most cultures at one time or another.

**Tapestry, Egypt, 4th century**
A Romano-Egyptian tapestry has a common arrangement of four central roundels surrounded by a border of smaller roundels. The design, depicting animals and hunters, reflects Roman mosaic floor patterns. The four main roundels are subtly linked by twists in the pattern.

**Silk, Persian Empire, c.600–1000**
The yellowish ground and dark green patterns are characteristic of this period of Persian textiles. The symmetrical decoration consists of two roundels containing a confronted pair of lions and palm trees. A stylised tree divides the panel symmetrically.

**Velvet, Burma, 19th century**
This *kalaga* or hanging has appliqué pattern in cotton, silver-wire embroidery and sequins. The appliqué design of the Burmese zodiac sign *Danu* (the archer) in the centre is surrounded by delicate foliate and figurative borders.

**Carpet, Persia, 1909**
The central field of this hand-knotted woollen piece was woven from a full-size cartoon inspired by a painting by Antoine Watteau entitled *Fêtes Vénitiennes*. In this case the circle is acting as a frame for the design.

**Wool and linen, Sweden, early 20th century**
A heavily formalised folk design in which the figure in the circle appears to be engaged with an angel, with another angel hovering above. The roundel is surrounded with stylised flowers, with three initials inside the top of the circle, possibly those of the maker or user.

# Toiles

### 18th–21st Century

A toile is the term for a textile that shows patterns based on pictorial representations of scenes or people. Toile designs are typically associated with depictions of contemporary life, classical antiquity, politics, the Orient and country living. In this selection the emphasis is on the representation of people, as opposed to landscape, showing the range of imagery used in the period c.1760–1860, the heyday of toile production in England and France. The imagery used may be simply decorative or in some cases may have a propaganda function or a didactic element as well.

**Linen and cotton, England, c.1766**

A plate-printed fustian furnishing fabric depicting scenes from a play by David Garrick, *Lethe, or Aesop in The Shades*, first performed in 1740. The figures are taken from paper prints, and the textile was probably designed at about the time of the command performance of 1766.

**Cotton, France, c.1816**
This contemporary fashion pattern features pictorial scenes in medallions. Its images commemorate famous Parisian buildings and include the Pont Neuf, the Louvre and the Pantheon, all framed on a diaper background that reflects the grand interiors of the print rooms.

**Cotton, England, c.1820**
'Scenes representing the British Isles', and English toile designed to be used as a furnishing fabric. In the tradition of didactic and propaganda textiles popular in the early 19th century, it shows four repeated vignettes of the nations that comprised the British Isles.

**Cotton, France, c.1825**
Produced in Nantes – an important printing centre in this period – this plate-printed furnishing fabric depicts four heroines connected with a war. The lower left scene is from the Greek War of Independence (1821–32); a massacre of Greeks by Ottoman Turks can be seen in the background.

**Linen, Scotland, 2008**
This contemporary take on the toile tradition by Glasgow-based designers Timorous Beasties shows how historical pattern can be updated. It features London landmarks, including Tower Bridge and the 'Gherkin'; white trees and figures in the foreground offer a more human scale.

# Lace

### 17th–18th Century

The technique of bobbin lace-making uses lengths of thread, which are wound on bobbins to assist in controlling the pattern. The work is kept in place with pins set in a lace pillow, which has the design on it for the lace-maker to follow. The pattern may include toile material, net grounds, braids, and fillings, depending on the particular design being worked. Lace pattern may be derived from any number of sources, but these particular examples seem to reflect a painterly influence in their execution.

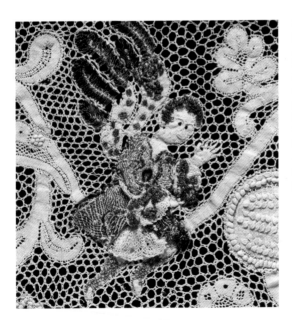

**Lace, detail, northern Italy, late 17th century**
A bobbin-lace flounce in linen and silver thread depicting an angel. an image heavy with symbolism, both as the link between God and the world, and as a warning sign of the Divine Presence. As messengers, angels are always bearers of good tidings.

**Lace, detail, northern Italy, late 17th century**

A male figure on part of a bobbin-lace flounce has been worked carefully into this design, posing in relaxed style on one of the formalised pieces of foliage that form the main pattern.

**Lace, detail, Italy, late 17th century**

This portion from a panel of bobbin-lace shows a man and woman in the centre of a floral border. Fashionably dressed and posed in courtly style, they are delicately posed on the outscale stems that surround them.

**Lace, detail, Italy, late 17th century**

Part of a Milanese bobbin-lace panel showing a hunter with a spear and his dog: the hunted deer just showing on the left of the detail. The hunting imagery speaks of both the spiritual quest in the tracking and the destruction of ignorance in the kill.

**Lace, detail, Flanders, early 18th century**

An exotically dressed individual with a spectacular costume and hat parades across this bobbin-lace panel. He holds an umbrella in his right hand and a novelty in his left. The style has some overtones of the contemporary taste for Chinoiserie.

# Human Form

### 17th–20th Century

Textile patterns that use images based on the human figure have featured in this book already. This selection looks at how patterns have been created with parts of the body, either in an abstracted way or rather more literally.

In some cases the abstraction removes the image from any sense of reality, whereas in other cases recognition of the particular body part is simple and sometimes amusing. In all cases the logic of the pattern-making can be seen in a relatively simple repeat of the established motif.

**Silk, detail, Persia, c.1600–1625**
The interest in this figure lies in the way in which it was altered after it was first made. The ewer and wine cup held by the figure in the original were changed to vases of simple flowers. Similarly, a caste mark and nose ring were also added later.

**Silk, France, 1938**
Designed by the Surrealist poet and film-maker Jean Cocteau, this printed silk crêpe dress fabric has an all-over pattern that shows a woman's profile unravelling into loops and ribbons. The effect is slightly bizarre.

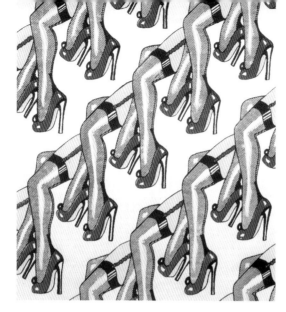

**Satin, Britain, 1973**
'Legs', designed by Jane Wealleans and produced by OK Textiles, a screen-printed furnishing fabric that appears to poke fun at 'good taste' through its postmodern irony and the use of a 'commercial' and slightly risqué image.

**Satin, England, 1973**
This screen-printed furnishing fabric features a pattern made up of fingers, raspberries and lips. The multiple repeat is a half-dropped simple image set in vertical panels. There is an exciting vibrancy about the pattern that owes much to contemporary graphic design.

**(Unknown), Britain, 1983**
Designers Timney Fowler have been very successful in adapting classical architectural and sculptural imagery to textile patterns. This pattern, designed as part of their neoclassical collection, shows vertical columns of classical sculpted emperors' heads, which were printed like engravings in black on white.

# Introduction

Conversational or pictorial patterns are a group of designs that might be called conversation-provoking. The name encourages the idea that the design can begin a conversation, owing to its inherent interest. The range of patterns in this genre is enormous, and includes novelty, prints, images of people in landscapes, and mythological and allegorical scenes such as those found in tapestry and toiles. This selection also incorporates maps and heraldic images.

**Silk, fragment, Byzantium, c.770–899**
This 'Lion Strangler' design depicts a man wrestling a lion, representing the theme of man's victory over animals. The image can be variously understood as representing that of the Christian figures, Samson or David, or the classical hero Hercules.

**Cotton, detail, India, c.1720–50**
This detail of a chintz *palampore* or hanging, filled with exquisitely rendered flowers, is part of a larger design entitled 'Nature Being Crowned by Love'. The design reflects an interest in the natural world that was a feature of the 18th-century Enlightenment.

**Wool, detail, England, c.1839**

Part of a woven waistcoat with hand-stitched cotton designs. It commemorates the Eglinton Tournament of 1839, which was a re-enactment of a medieval joust set up as a deliberate Romantic statement, created in the face of extensive contemporary social change.

**Cotton, England, 1920**

Entitled 'Alice in Wonderland', this is a roller-printed chintz furnishing fabric designed by C.F.A. Voysey. He designed matching tiles and wallpaper using some of Sir John Tenniel's original illustrations for *Alice in Wonderland* and *Through the Looking Glass*, which he tinted and ordered into a patterned landscape.

**Cotton, France, 1927**

Clowns and circus imagery used in patterns such as this, were a favourite choice for children's clothing. This example is a lively rendering of typical clowning antics, complete with face paint and silly costumes.

# Sports

### 19th–20th Century

Although sporting images have been used on fabric for a considerable time, it was with the development of participatory and spectator sports from the end of the 19th century that another set of pattern-making exemplars became popular with the textile designer. Whether for men or women, furnishing or apparel, sporting images made ideal energetic conversational patterns. Featuring individual sporting activities or groups at play, sporting patterns often give an impression of movement and excitement that reflect the nature of the subject.

**Cotton, England, c.1818–24**

This roller-printed fabric features a classic image of the hunt set in a detailed depiction of the English countryside. Hunting scenes were popular because they depicted a bucolic ideal of country life, and this sort of scene can be found on many toile designs.

**Cotton, France, 1882**

A two-colour roller-print depicting horses jumping angled fences in varying poses. Although the pattern is heavily stylised, the interaction between horse and jockey seems lively, and there is a sense of energetic movement in the pattern.

**Silk, USA, 1927**

Unsurprisingly, the pattern on this printed dress fabric is called 'A Game of Tennis'. The designer, Helen Wills Moody, was a celebrated American tennis player as well as an amateur artist. This pattern was part of a range that was intended to depict contemporary American life.

**Silk, USA, 1940s**

This small, simple image of a fisherman with vast fish jumping around his boat was produced as a pattern to be used on ties. Much of the energy and variety comes from the use of reverse images, so that both fisherman and fish appear in silhouette.

**Cotton, USA, 1954**

A light-hearted and heavily abstracted printed design called 'Kites and Mites' depicting stickmen figures and variously shaped flying kites. This sort of pattern, although appropriate for a child's room, also owes something to the work of modern artists such as Paul Klee and Joan Miró.

# Pictorial Scenes

### 14th–20th Century

The conversational pattern type has used pictorial scenes of people for a long time. There is no doubt that humans have a fascination with their own image, so this is a highly suitable subject for pattern-making. The range encompasses stylised human figures, both real and imaginary that may tell a story or commemorate a deed often in a fixed panel design rather than as part of a repeating effect. These scenes are particularly useful for hangings and cushions, which offer a flat surface area to display the pattern, which are painstakenly made up.

**Velvet, England, c.1320–40**
A decorative panel to be sewn onto an alb, this piece elaborately embroidered, shows scenes from the life of the Virgin, each set within a Gothic arch. It demonstrates the vigorous narrative style that was a feature of *opus anglicanum* embroidery, which was often executed by nuns.

**Linen canvas, England, mid 17th century**
Worked as the front of a cushion cover, this wool and silk embroidery shows two scenes from the story of Abraham in the Old Testament. Biblical images were popular in the 17th century and were often derived from contemporary illustrated stories. The quality of the detail is remarkable.

**Cotton, England, c.1780**
This rural scene with a group of men deep in conversation as an angel hovers above them is the principal motif on a plate-printed fabric. The significance of the pattern is not clear, although biblical scenes rendered in contemporary dress were not unknown in the late 18th century.

**Carpet, France, 1781**
A hand-knitted woollen carpet depicting Adam and Eve beneath a central panel illustrating the story of Jacob's dream. The inscription – *hilfe wirt gott ferner schicken meinen feinden zum verdus* – translates as 'God will continue to send help in despite mine enemies'.

# Pictorial Scenes

**Linen, detail, England, early 18th century**
The subject of this sampler, embroidered with silk and metal thread in cross, satin, split and chain stitch is Queen Anne, who ruled from 1702 to 1714. The square or rectanglar shape of the typical sampler made it suitable for framing and displaying prints and paintings.

**Linen, Sweden, 1770–1820**
A delightful example of a marriage textile produced in southern Sweden as part of a young woman's dowry. Such woven textiles usually have black or dark-brown backgrounds, and are ornamented with small pictorial vignettes, surrounded by freely interpreted flower imagery.

**Silk, India, 19th century**
An embroidered wall hanging or *chakla* worked in silk. The squared grid contains nine vignettes bounded by floral patterns. Within these borders, stylised human figures are represented at various tasks, alongside many kinds of animals and birds.

**Cotton, USA, 1930**
Ruth Reeves designed this printed monk's cloth furnishing fabric entitled 'Play Boy' in 1930. She trained with the artist Fernand Léger during the 1920s and was influenced by his Cubist work, as is evident by the bold simplicity of the outlines here.

**Cotton, detail, Indonesia, date unknown**
A batik cloth from the north coast of the Indonesian island of Java. The detail depicts fantastical figures carrying banners and a house or carnival float covered with panels or banners. The pattern is filled in with other bizarre figures, all of which have their own symbolic meanings.

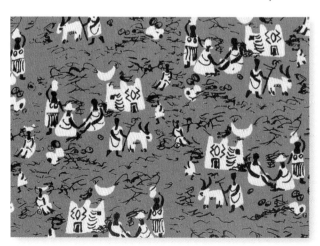

**Rayon, Britain, 1948**
Designed by Julian Trevelyan, this printed material was produced for Ascher of London. Trevelyan was a painter and was strongly associated with Surrealism in Britain. His work often has a rather childlike quality and the scene on this material has a pleasing simplicity.

# Hunting Scenes

### 15th–20th Century

The use of hunting scenes in textile design has a long and distinguished history. Some of the earliest-known textiles depict images of lion hunts, while later patterns frequently show the hunter pitted against the powerful wild animal. Other examples in the genre include patterns made around bird catching, falconry and horse racing. In some cases, the figures in these patterns are dressed very finely, making the whole event seem more social than destructive. The styles of representation vary greatly in this selection, but the imagery remains clear.

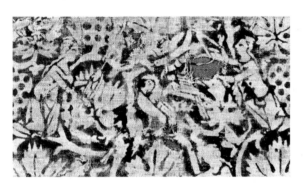

**Linen, panel, Flanders, c.1420–30**
This panel is printed with a pattern depicting figures working bird snares amongst oversized leaf, flower and fruit motifs. The uneven outline may reflect the results of the block-cutting process. The scene is highly animated, with a real sense of activity.

**Tapestry, detail, southern Netherlands, c.1435–45**
The famous Devonshire Hunting Tapestries, woven with wool and natural dyes, depict various hunting scenes. This pictorial detail taken from the larger 'Boar and Bear Hunt' piece shows a crouching man with dogs, a fashionable lady and a horse.

**Satin, England, c.1600**

An embroidered cushion that depicts various country pursuits, including falconry and stag hunting, set amongst an orchard scene with other birds and figures. The design has been carefully worked out to fill the space available, although little or no attention has been paid to realistic comparative scale.

**Satin, detail, India, c.1605–27**

Scene from a hunting coat, made from satin and covered with designs of animals and flowers that are embroidered in silks. The graphic image of a lion with its prey makes clear reference to the use of this garment for wearing during a hunt.

**Cotton, USA, 1930**

One of America's best-known steeplechases, the Aiken Drag is located in South Carolina and is celebrated in 'Aiken Drag', a furnishing fabric designed by Ruth Reeves. The colours of the uniform (green with chamois collar and white breeches) are reflected in the patterning of the fabric.

# Worldwide Mythological

### 19th–20th Century

Mythology, legends and folk tales are narratives involving gods and other entities from the distant past; legends in particular are stories about the past, often focused on human heroes and heroines; folk and fairy tales are stories that lack any definite historical setting, frequently featuring fairies, witches and animal characters with human attributes. The value of these images is that they have a certain universality and that the designer can interpret them as he or she wishes.

**Silk, detail, China, 19th century**
This back view of a *kesi* cut-silk tapestry robe shows the detail of a dragon, against a heavily patterned background of clouds and sea. The dragon is the symbol of the emperor, and in imperial China was considered to have celestial, law-giving and creative powers.

**Linen, Russia, 19th century**
The main feature of this worsted and silk embroidered towel is the two-headed eagle in the principal frieze which, in Byzantine heraldry, represents secular and religious sovereignty of the emperor. Since appropriated by other cultures, it is now associated with the Russian imperial empire.

**Silk, cotton and wool, England, late 1890s**

This woven double-cloth, designed by Harry Napper, depicts Pan-like creatures playing pipes in a forest scene. Pan was the god of shepherds. The sinuous, swirling lines are typical of the imagery associated with Art Nouveau.

**Cotton, detail, Japan, 20th century**

Part of a fisherman's celebratory robe with stencilled decoration, this piece shows a fisherman in his boat alongside a sea-dragon and surrounded by other symbols and references. The dragon lives in the sea, where it is linked to rain-making and lightning.

**Cotton, Britain, c.1930s**

The painter and designer Nancy Nicholson produced this printed textile entitled 'The Unicorn'. In the Middle Ages the unicorn was a symbol of power and magnificence, but in this pattern it is used entirely decoratively, its large shadow seems to overpower the scene.

# Maps

### 16th–20th Century

Maps used as decorative images vary between accurate representations of areas of land, and fanciful stylisations of imagined views. During World War II, aircrew carried maps printed on silk in case of a crash landing, but most map patterns on textiles have been produced solely for their decorative value. This cross-section covers a wide range of periods and places. Some of the examples are detailed and can be read topographically; others are purely impressionistic and simply give a feel for the area being depicted.

**Wool and silk, fragment, England, late 16th century**

Made at the Sheldon workshops, this piece from a panel shows a map of an area in south London. Symbols and pictures have been borrowed from a printed source to complement the work, helping to enliven the map through inserted and stressed details.

**Linen and wool, England, 1780**
Samplers were initially intended as
reference works for embroiderers.
Later they were used to demonstrate
both academic and needlework talents.
In this case, the pupil or her teacher drew
the map onto the canvas and it was then
embroidered, showcasing both skills.

**Wool, detail, India, late 19th century**
A novelty 'map' shawl, intended more for
display than for wear. It is decorated with
embroidery in coloured wools, and depicts
the town of Srinagar, in Kashmir, in a
scenic panorama with details of the
buildings and surroundings.

**Wool, detail, India, late 19th century**
An embroidered Kashmiri shawl decorated
with a map of Srinagar, but in greater
detail than the example of the top right.
It shows individual buildings and details
of the river with its boats, bridges, and
processions of houseboats.

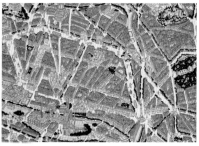

**Silk, USA, 1927**
This printed crêpe de Chine dress fabric
called 'Map of Paris', was designed by
Ralph Barton. The Exposition des Arts
Décoratifs of 1925 had an enormous
impact on American designers, who
responded with designs that reflected
the mood of the time.

# Figures in Toiles

### 18th–19th Century

Toile is the generic name for the scenic, copperplate-printed designs produced on cotton cloth, including those influenced by the productions of Christophe-Philippe Oberkampf at Jouy-en-Josas, France. The attraction of toiles was based on the pictorial representations they offered. Their scenes of contemporary life, classical antiquity, politics, the Orient and country living were an antidote to the formality of some court-influenced interiors. Toiles were initially used as summer drapes and curtains to replace heavier winter hangings, but their popularity meant that they were soon available for all kinds of furnishings and hangings.

**Cotton, England, c.1770–80**
Plate-printed fabric by Nixon & Co., which has been made into a curtain. This rural scene with ruins was printed using an engraved copper plate introduced in the 1750s. The printing process enabled the maker to achieve greater fineness of detail and delicacy of drawing and much larger pattern repeats.

**Cotton, France, c.1760–1800**
A roller-printed furnishing fabric with representations of the life of Robinson Crusoe on his desert island. Produced in Jouy-en-Josas, it not only proves the widespread popularity of the story, but also the use of literature as a pattern source.

**Cotton, England, late 18th century**
Politically inspired patterns were uncommon in toiles, but here George Washington drives a chariot, in which sits an allegorical figure of America holding a plaque inscribed with 'American Independence 1776'; and Athene accompanies Benjamin Franklin and the figure of Liberty.

**Cotton, England, c.1816–20**
A large-scale toile repeat showing an enormous range of imagery, including flora, fauna, charioteers, Britannia, rocks, angels and Chinoiserie. The meaning of this attractive but bizarre assortment is known, but was probably intended to demonstrate the skill of the engraver.

**Cotton, France, c.1800–50**
A typical toile, with a rural scene depicting idealised country life. This detail shows the farmer and his wife, with animals and farm produce and equipment. The lower part of the repeat features a woman in classical dress holding a baby.

# Landscape

### 16th–20th Century

Closely associated with an interest in nature is the taste for patterns that depict landscape scenes. The examples here offer a range of eye-catching elements, either of content or design, that pull them into the conversational category. As with most other patterns, landscapes can be abstracted to a few essential elements that engage the eye, or they can attempt true-to life representations of the real thing.

**Silk, Persia, 16th century**

A lampas textile of silk and metal threads, with a repeat pattern of motifs derived from Persian miniature paintings of the time, including cypress trees, fantastic birds, a fish pool, a rocky outcrop, and a deer lying at rest.

**Carpet, India, c.1640**

Unusually, the coat of arms of William Fremlin, a senior official in the East India Company, has been introduced as part of the pattern here, appearing either side of the lower half within the Persian-style composition of exotic animals fighting against a background of flowers.

**Linen, Ottoman Empire, 19th century**
Embroidered with silk and metal thread, this towel border depicts a stylised landscape with a building surrounded with tall trees, all centred within an arcaded framework. A frieze of flora and a sun shape between each arcade complete the pattern.

**Cotton, England, 1904**
Designed by the Silver Studios, this panel intended as a cushion, depicts a rural scene in the Arts and Crafts manner. The pattern is in the style of C.F.A. Voysey, one of the most popular of all British Arts and Crafts designers.

**Cotton, England, 1976**
Jennie Foley designed this screen-printed furnishing fabric entitled 'Country Walk'. The pattern depicts an arable landscape with trees and a fence, setting a mood through its colour scheme and the particular stylisation of trees, land texture and hedging.

# Coats-of-Arms

### 16th–17th Century

The use of coats of arms in textile patterning generally makes reference to the patron who commissioned the work. Because coats of arms were originally used to identifiy individuals, they had particular legal purposes, so were strictly regulated. Their application to domestic objects such as cushions, carpets, silver and even stained glass was not only a means of identification, but also a way of demonstrating the lineage of a family and thus its place in society. Although the examples shown here are English, heraldry in various forms is found all around the world.

**Linen, England, 16th century**
An embroidered cushion cover displaying the arms of Warneford. The combination of heraldic motifs of the family and the representation of flora, all fitted into a frame border, is not unusual and was used extensively in canvas work. Long cushions were ideal for such designs.

## Tapestry, detail, England, c.1588

Although the ferocious boar is the first thing to catch the eye in this panel from a large map made at the Sheldon workshops for Ralph Sheldon, the family coat of arms just above it is conspicuously laid over part of a map of the local area.

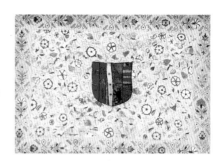

## Linen, England, 1592

Used as a commemorative cushion cover celebrating the marriage of Bernard Grenville and Elizabeth Bevill in 1592, this piece centres their crest on a ground of flowers. Prosperous families often included their crest on household items to demonstrate their rank.

## Canvas, England, c.1600

Slips like this are small, embroidered motifs that were intended to be cut out and applied to a luxurious backing fabric. Embroidered in silk and metal thread, this example depicts the conjoined coats of arms of Fitzwilliam and Sydney, indicating a husband and wife.

## Linen, England, 17th century

An embroidered cushion cover in coloured silks and metal thread bearing both the royal arms of James II, and the name of Mary Hulton, who was the embroiderer. The flowers, foliage and insects in the pattern reveal the interest taken in the natural world at this time.

# Around the World

**18th–19th Century**

This collection of patterns from around the world represents the typical, and at the same time stereotypical, imagery that conveys a nation to other people. Such images may consist of no more than a handful of clichéd motifs; others may take a famous monument or tradition and centre a design on it. Hawaiian casual shirts, the paisley motif associated with India and the tie-dyes of Southeast Asia are all examples of patterns with associated national identity. While the patterns may be of particular significance to the originators, they often lose most of all their meaning in translation.

**Silk and cotton, Mexico, c.1775–1800**
Interesting combinations of pattern motifs make up this shawl. The main area is divided into bands by stripes and chevrons, leaving a space for sets of pictorial images of women, dancers and uniformed soldiers, linked by swagged motifs.

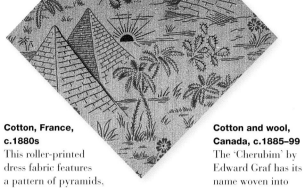

### Cotton, France, c.1880s

This roller-printed dress fabric features a pattern of pyramids, palms, cactus and sun, reflecting an interest in ancient Egypt, which began in France in Napoleonic times. Taken together the elements represent Egypt through association, the imagery is stylised, possibly unrealistic and certainly naïve.

### Cotton and wool, Canada, c.1885–99

The 'Cherubim' by Edward Graf has its name woven into both faces of this coverlet. Graf was a professional weaver who designed his patterns incorporating both old and new motifs. Woven coverlets are particularly associated with North America.

### Wool, Hungary, 1936

The *szur* or mantle is a Magyar coat that was traditionally worn over the shoulders, cape-style. This one is sumptuously decorated with embroidery and cutwork felt appliqué. The whole thing, including the applied decoration, was made exclusively by male tailors.

### Cotton, detail, USA, 1950s

This screenprinted tablecloth with a highly stereotypical image of Mexico was acceptable as a decorative pattern in the 1950s and is widely collected for its kitch value today. However, images such as these would probably not feature in any contemporary design.

# Glossary

**ABSTRACT** Patterns that have been adapted so as to be no longer representative, figurative or naturalistic.

**ACANTHUS** Leaves of the Mediterranean acanthus plant, originally used for scrolls and ornament in Classical architecture, have been widely used in art and design since the Renaissance. Associated with enduring life, the plant is traditionally displayed at funeral celebrations.

**ALLEYWAYS** Unintentional spaces that create unwanted lines in a design.

**ALL-OVER** A design that involves a whole area being decorated with many motifs distributed in a composed way. The design can be based on floral, naturalistic or abstract motifs.

**APPLIQUÉ** Pieces of fabric cut and shaped and then stitched to a ground fabric to create a design or pattern.

**ARABESQUE** A design featuring symmetrical curvilinear shapes, or branches, often with added motifs, especially popular in the Renaissance.

**ARGYLE** A design of variously coloured diamond-shaped blocks that are usually crossed by lines that overlay a single coloured ground.

**ART DECO** A style of design popular in the 1920s and 1930s associated with stylised

motifs including geometrics and florals.

**ART NOUVEAU** A style of decorative art from the late 19th/early 20th century that was particularly associated with sinuous flowing lines among other abstracted or formalised motifs.

**ARTS AND CRAFTS** A late 19th-century design movement that encouraged craftsmanship and quality in design. Particularly associated with William Morris.

**BALANCED DESIGN** A design that has no obvious gaps, breaks or lines that might be created by a predominance of one motif over another.

**BALANCED STRIPES** A pattern featuring a selection of – usually smaller – stripes evenly arranged around a centre stripe.

**BAROQUE** A 17th-century style associated with exuberant, complex and expansive decoration.

**BASKETWEAVE** A plain weave with two or more warp yarns that interlace with the same balance of filler yarns, so that the fabric has a basket-like surface effect.

**BATIK** A resist-dyeing process that uses wax to inhibit the dye, thus making a pattern.

**BATISTE** A semi-transparent plain-weave fabric made from fine cotton yarns.

**BAUHAUS** An influential German design school in the early 20th century that had a major impact on design thinking.

**BINGATA** A type of stencil-dyed fabric originating from the island of Okinawa from the Ryukyu Kingdom period (14th century). It is frequently brightly coloured and features various patterns, often depicting natural subjects such as fish, water and flowers.

**BIRD'S-EYE** A term for a fabric with a surface pattern effect of small, uniform spots that suggest birds' eyes.

**BLOCK PRINT** A printing process using carved wooden blocks that are applied directly to the fabric surface.

**BLOTCH** A name for a screen used in printing that fills in the ground remaining after the full design has been printed. This makes the fabric's background colour.

**BOTANICAL** Any pattern that uses a style derived from botanical illustrations, especially closely observed and realistically represented natural forms.

**BROCATELLE** A damask with a plain or satin-weave ground in which a design is woven in a satin or twill; the different weaves create a subtle contrasting effect.

**BUFFALO CHECK** A bold check pattern made up of blocks

of two or three contrasting colours. Reds and blacks in a twill weave are often used.

**BURN-OUT OR ETCHED PRINTING** A printing process whereby an acid solution is applied to dissolve fibres from a fabric woven from blended yarns. The pattern appears in shadow outline on the surface of the material.

**CARTOON** A full-sized drawing on heavy-duty paper. Cartoons can be designs for a work in tapestry, or another medium.

**CARTOUCHE** A decorative motif imitating carved ornamental panels with scroll formations on the edges. It may be used for specific parts of a pattern to help to create a repeat more easily.

**CASEMENT CLOTH** A lightweight textile made in a combination of fibres, usually dyed in light neutral colours.

**CELTIC KNOT** A decorative motif derived from early Celtic pattern-making that uses interlacing ribbons that appear to flow seamlessly together.

**CHEVRON** A herringbone or zigzag pattern that runs horizontally across a surface.

**CHINA BLUE** The application of indigo dyes to cloth was developed in England in the 18th century. Its name comes from the finished effect, which is similar to blue-and-white Chinese ceramics.

**CHINOISERIE** The use of Chinese influenced design motifs in Western decorative arts.

**CHINTZ** Originally, a name for the painted or stained cotton cloths imported from India; now, a name for a glazed plainweave cotton cloth with a hand-spun fine warp and a coarser slack twist weft, fast-printed with designs in a number of colours, generally not fewer than five.

**CLASSICISM** The use of designs base on proportion and symmetry derived from ancient Greek and Roman models.

**COTTON** A natural fibre that grows in the seed pod of the cotton plant. There are four main types of cotton, namely American Upland, Egyptian, Sea Island and Asiatic. Cotton is generally very elastic, able to withstand high temperatures, easily washable and takes dyes very well.

**COVERAGE** A term to identify the area of a textile that is covered by motifs. It is the opposite of negative space.

**CRASH** A coarse woven fabric made with thick uneven yarns that create a textured surface.

**CRÊPE** A fabric with an irregular and crinkly surface mainly used for dress fabrics but has been employed as a furnishing fabric on occasion.

**CREWEL** Embroidery of fine

two-ply worsted woollen yarns on twilled union fabric.

**CROQUIS** A sketch in watercolour on detail paper for a design idea that has only been partially realised or put into repeat.

**DAMASK** A cloth of silk or wool woven by Jacquard loom, in which a pattern of ornamental stylised motifs is woven in one colour, but the weave gives a tone-on-tone effect.

**DIAPER** A repeat pattern based on lozenge or diamond shapes.

**DIRECTIONAL** A pattern that only works in one direction.

**DOBBY** Small symmetrical figures in a regular repeat, formed by the adjustment of the harness attachment (chain) on a plain loom.

**DOG'S-TOOTH** A pattern of checks formed by four-pointed stars, which is sometimes also called hound's-tooth.

**EPINGLÉ** A special high loop velvet-type fabric, often called a moquette, produced in Belgium on wire looms. Usually, epinglés are made from the highest grades of cotton, producing a very soft but durable fabric.

**ETHNIC** A particular design characteristic associated with a specific nationality.

**FIGURATIVE** A pattern that uses the human figure as the basis for the design.

# Glossary

**FLAX** The raw material for linen yarns. It is derived from the stalk of the *Linum* plant. It is a long fibre with an off-white or tan colour and has brilliant lustre. It is one of the strongest vegetable fibres and is very absorbent. Although easy to crease, it is a highly useful yarn.

**FLEUR-DE-LYS** A stylised lily motif with three or four petals. Originally a medieval heraldic symbol associated with purity.

**FOULARD** A plain or twill-weave fabric made from silk or rayon yarns.

**FUGITIVE** Dyes that allow the colour to be easily removed, or that fade quickly. In contrast, if the colour is quite robust when subjected to repeated washing or to strong light, it is called a fast colour.

**GARLAND** Classical motif made from flowers and foliage, which, when joined at each end, becomes a wreath, or when draped becomes a festoon.

**GINGHAM** Cotton cloth printed or woven with small checks that are formed by stripes of the same colour.

**GREEK KEY** An architectural pattern of interlocking lines and right angles that is used for borders.

**GROTESQUE** A motif that combines a number of images of human figures, animals, foliage, etc., often in a columnar form. It is based on a Roman original found in a grotto.

**GROUND** Another name for the surface area of a textile.

**GUILLOCHE** A pattern made up from a repeating band of interlacing shapes, often forming circles.

**HALF-DROP REPEAT** A common method of creating a pattern repeat, in which the design is dropped halfway down the first area of pattern. The staggering of every other line of motifs makes an interesting pattern with fewer motifs, and avoids any deadening effect of having the same motif repeated over and over again at the same height.

**IKAT** A system of dyeing in which parts of the yarns to be woven are tied to resist the dye. When woven, the pattern is created from the mix of dyed and undyed threads.

**ISLAND PATTERN** A repeat motif that is isolated on a plain background cloth.

**JACQUARD LOOM** A mechanism that controls a series of perforated cards that are attached to the top of the loom. The mechanism lifts or lowers the warps so that the most complex designs are possible. Joseph Jacquard developed this revolutionary technique in France at the turn of the 19th century.

**KENTE** An African material made from narrow strips of woven cloth to form bold and vibrant patterns.

**KIMONO** An important Japanese garment made with straight seams and based on a standardised pattern. It is usually cut from a piece of cloth 12–13 metres (39–42ft) long and 36–7 cm (14–15in.) wide.

**LISERÉ** A type of fabric construction that involves the use of a supplementary warp. This warp can be used to add colour and detail in selected areas on the face of the fabric. Where the *liseré* effect is not seen on the face of the fabric, it is hidden along the back as loosely tacked 'floats'. The technique is often used for stripes.

**MADRAS** Originally fine cottons from India used for dress or shirting and usually featuring stripes, checks or plaids.

**MILLEFLEURS** A name that literally means 'a thousand flowers' in French. It is usually related to medieval tapestries that sport multi-flowered backgrounds.

**MOIRÉ** Fabric with an effect of spilt water, achieved by the application of extreme but uneven pressure from heated cylinders onto a folded and dampened ribbed material.

**MORDANT** A substance (usually a metallic compound) used to set dyes on textiles by forming an insoluble compound with the dye.

**MOSAIC** A design with many small pieces, used either to make up motifs or to create asymmetrical patterns.

**MOTIF** A decorative design element that, repeated, is often the basis for a full design.

**MUGHAL** A term referring to the empire that controlled India from the early 16th century, which covered a large part of the Indian subcontinent and was important in unifying government and trade. In cultural terms the merging of Persian culture with the native Indian traditions produced a wonderful flowering of art and design.

**NATURALISTIC** The representation of organic forms that are close enough to the real thing to be instantly recognisable.

**NEGATIVE SPACE** The space that remains between motifs on a patterned surface.

**OFFSET** A reference to the degree of linear or angular displacement of part of a pattern. It may refer to the amount or distance by which something is out of line. It may also be part of a counterbalancing scheme in a design.

**OGEE** An arch shape made up from a double curved line with both a convex and a concave part.

**OMBRÉE** A shadow-like effect that moves from light to dark and back again. It often has stripes that pass from open to closed and then reverse.

**OPTICAL ART** An abstract painting movement, the effects of which are much in pattern-making in the applied and decorative arts. Many of the patterns created play visual tricks and seem to move when looked at.

**OUTLINE QUILTING** A hand-guided quilting process in which the stitching trails the motifs of the design in a printed fabric, creating an embossed effect.

**PAISLEY** A highly stylised type of pattern with characteristic motifs of flowers and abstract forms. It originated in India and is widely used in both printed and woven fabrics.

**QUATREFOIL** A geometric form originally found in architecture. It consists of four arcs enclosed within a circle and separated by cusps. They are characteristic of Gothic stone or woodwork and are often used in decorative patterns to create a Gothic effect.

**RAILROAD** The method of turning a fabric in such a way that the selvedges are in a horizontal position. Some upholstery fabrics are designed like this so that they can be cut in the most economical way.

**RENAISSANCE** A major period of design innovation, from the 14th to the 17th centuries, that was based on a revival of classical learning and its applications.

**REPEAT** The means of planning a design so that it will fit repeatedly into a specified format. Each repeat is a unit containing a complete set of the different elements in the design. Repeats are referred to as drops: e.g. half-drop, quarter or third drop repeats.

**RESIST OR RESERVE PRINTING** The use of a dye-resistant substance in printing that leaves the background coloured after a washed finish.

**ROCOCO** A decorative style popular in the 18th century that used asymmetrical ornament based on shell-work, foliage and S-shaped curves.

**ROLLER PRINT** A process of continuous printing using engraved metal rollers.

**ROMAN STRIPES** Bright, wide stripes.

**SCALE** A reference to the size of a motif or pattern. Scaling up or down is potentially useful for differing applications of the pattern. A separate meaning refers to a specific fish-scale pattern.

# Glossary

**SCREENPRINTING** A hand-or machine-printing process, in which a stencilled screen held in a frame is positioned around fabric or paper and colour is applied with a squeegee, pressing it through the screen and onto the surface to be printed. A separate screen is required for each colour of the pattern.

**SHIBORU** A Japanese term for a method of dyeing cloth with a pattern by binding, stitching, folding, twisting or compressing the fabric beforehand to leave areas inaccessible to the dye. Also known as tie-dye.

**SIDE REPEAT** A design that repeats itself horizontally.

**SPANDREL** An architectural term for the triangular space between the outer curve of an arch and its vertical/horizontal framing.

**SQUARE REPEAT** A pattern that repeats in line with itself – that is, the repeats are side by side.

**STRIÉ** A striped design in which a directional effect is created by restrained deviations in colour or surface effect.

**TABBY** A plain-weave construction in which each warp thread passes over and under a single weft thread. The threads of the warp and weft are of the same size and set at even distances apart, resulting in a balanced weave.

**TABLE PRINTING** A form of screenprinting in which the cloth is stretched and secured to the top of a table and the screens are moved down the table either by hand or machine, pattern repeat by pattern repeat.

**TAPESTRY** The name for both a technique and its product in which a piece of fabric is woven on a loom by hand following a design. The weft threads are used in the design where necessary, but are not used across the whole width.

**TIE-DYE** A method of resist dyeing in which the material to be dyed is first folded into a pattern and tied or bound with string or rubber bands. The ties resist the penetration of dye, resulting in a pattern on the dyed fabric when they are removed at the end of the process.

**TROMPE-L'OEIL** An image made to create the illusion that the objects it depicts are actually there, in three dimensions.

**TURNOVER** A pattern in which the design is flipped over horizontally or vertically, often seen in ogee or damask patterns.

**TWILL** A basic weave in which the filler threads pass over two or more ends in a regular progression, creating a diagonal pattern.

**VOLUTE** Originally a volute was an architectural term for the spiral ornament that was placed on each side of an Ionic capital. Volutes are also referred to as scroll ends and may originally have been a representation of a ram's horn, or simply a geometric formulation. Two-dimensional volute shapes have become part of the pattern-maker's repertoire.

**WARP** The threads of a cloth that run lengthwise in a loom.

**WARP PRINT** A fabric where the design has been printed on the warp before it has been woven. This results in a pattern with an indistinct, soft-edged image, similar to the effect of Impressionist art.

**WEFT** The threads that run across a cloth and are interlaced over and under the warps.

**YARN-DYED** Refers to textiles that have been woven with yarns that have been dyed prior to weaving. Most superior textiles are yarn-dyed.

**YUZEN** A technique of dyeing silk fabric in which rice-paste is applied to areas which are not to be dyed. The name comes from Japanese painter Miyazaki Yuzen, who invented the process, and was associated with his designs using the technique produced in the mid 18th century.

# Resources

## Books

EDWARDS, C. (2007), *Encyclopaedia of Furnishing Textiles and Soft Furnishings*, London: Lund Humphries

GILLOW, J. AND SENTANCE, B. (1999), *World Textiles*, London: Thames and Hudson

HARRIS, J. (1993), *5000 Years of Textiles*, London: British Museum Press

ISSETT, R. (2007), *Print, Pattern and Colour*, London: Batsford

JENKINS, D. (ed.), (2003), *The Cambridge History of Western Textiles*, Cambridge: Cambridge University Press, 2 vols

JOYCE, C. (1997), *Textile Design: The Complete Guide to Printed Textiles for Apparel and Home*, New York: Watson-Guptill

MELLER, S. AND ELFFERS, J. (2002), *Textile Designs: 200 Years of Patterns for Printed Fabrics Arranged by Motif, Colour, Period and Design*, London: Thames and Hudson

MONTGOMERY, F. (1984), *Textiles in America 1650–1870*, New York and London: Norton

NYLANDER, J.C. (1983), *Fabrics for Historic Buildings*, Washington DC: Preservation Press

PAINE, M. (1990), *Textile Classics: A Complete Guide to Furnishing Fabrics and their Uses*, London: Mitchell Beazley

SCHOESER, M. (1989), *English and American Textiles: From 1790 to the Present*, London: Thames and Hudson

SCHOESER. M. (2003), *World Textiles: A Concise History*, London: Thames and Hudson

TORTORA, P.G. AND MERKEL, R.S. (1996), *Fairchild's Dictionary of Textiles*, 7th ed., New York: Fairchild

## Museums

### United Kingdom

Museum of Costume, Bath

Royal Scottish Museum, Edinburgh

Bankfield Museum, Halifax

British Museum, London

Victoria and Albert Museum, London

Whitworth Gallery, Manchester

### North America

Museum of Fine Arts, Boston

The Art Institute, Chicago

Los Angeles County Museum of Art, Los Angeles

Brooklyn Museum, New York

Cooper Hewitt Museum, New York

Metropolitan Museum, New York

Museum of Art, Philadelphia

Royal Ontario Museum, Toronto

Textile Museum of Canada, Toronto

Smithsonian Institution, Washington

The Textile Museum, Washington

Colonial Williamsburg Foundation, Williamsburg

Winterthur Museum, Winterthur

### France

Musées des Tissus et des Arts Décoratifs, Lyon

Musée de l'Impression sur Etoffes, Mulhouse

# Index

**A**

abstract patterns 9, 55, 146–65, 246
acanthus leaves 45, 83, 93, 103, 246
Aesthetic Movement 69, 96, 97
Africa
  influence on European design 35, 46, 154, 203
  'strip cloth' 186
air travel motifs 182–3
Algeria 29
*Alice in Wonderland* 225
all-over designs 246
  floral 60–1
alleyways 246
Alsace 99, 204
altar frontals 35, 36
Anderson and Sheppard 201
Andrada, Madame 150
angels 207, 220
animals
  dogs 154, 221
  elephants 25, 37, 82, 84, 100–1
  horses 82, 98–9, 227
  lions 83, 118, 119, 217, 224, 232, 233
  rabbits 82, 83
  squirrels 83
  tortoises 125, 133
  *see also* birds; insects; marine life; mythological beasts
Anne, Queen of England 230
appliqué 246
arabesques 13, 104, 105, 108, 112, 246
architectural motifs 178–81
Ardabil Carpet, the 168
Argyle designs 246
arms, coats of 16, 240, 242–3
Art Deco 246
  designs 15, 46, 47, 53, 59, 80, 87, 89, 127, 130, 150, 153, 154–5, 173, 177, 179, 189, 196, 203

influence of 163
Art Nouveau 246
  designs 8, 31, 47, 59, 79, 80, 81, 235
  influence of 33, 39
Arts and Crafts 11, 14, 15, 17, 25, 47, 246
Ascher Ltd., London 39, 93, 180, 231
Audubon, John James 91, 92
Austria: Wiener Werkstätte designs 87, 193, 202
azaleas 121

**B**

balanced designs 246
balanced stripes 246
bamboo 8, 29, 48, 71, 120, 124, 125
Bannister Hall, Preston 74
Barbier, Georges 35
Baroque designs 246
Barron, Phyllis 187
Barton, Ralph 205, 237
baskets, floral 62–5
basketweave 192–3, 246
batik 231, 246
batiste 246
Baudouin, Christopher 68
Bauhaus 246
bed tents 34
bees 84, 85
Belgium
  lace 21, 53
  tapestry 17
Beluch region 129
Benares, Uttar Pradesh, India 188
*bingata* 91, 246
birds 16, 21, 23, 25, 33, 39, 46, 82, 90–7, 187
  cockerels 102
  cranes 82, 88, 94–5, 125, 133
  doves 155
  ducks 92
  geese/*hamsa* 94, 104
  ostriches 83
  parrots 143
  peacocks 81, 82, 96–7, 103, 122

pelicans 138
quails 90
swallows 93
swans 93
thrushes 25, 93
bird's-eye fabric 246
'bizarre' silks 49, 73
block printing 14, 246
blotch 246
bobbin lace 20, 21, 220, 221
*bodhi* 40
Bonfils, Robert 46, 47, 155
book cover designs 126
botanical patterns 246
  *see also* floral designs
*boteh* motifs 13, 31, 101, 104, 114–15, 116, 117
bouquets 66–7
Bouzois, Jean 144
Bradley, T. 133
Britain
  abstract designs 147, 163
  carpets 35
  conversational designs 225, 231, 235
  geometric designs 131, 139, 143
  grids & stripes 201
  human figures 213, 223
  objects as motifs 167, 171, 180
  stylised designs 111
  *see also* England; Scotland
brocading technique 12, 38, 110
brocatelle 12, 246
Bromley Hall 54
Brooks, Evelyn 145
Brown, Barbara 127, 145, 153, 189
Brown, Gregory 27, 130
Bruhns, Ivan da Silva 154
buffalo check 246–7
Bull, H.J. 141
Burma 96, 214, 215, 219
burn-out (etched) printing 247

Burne-Jones, Edward 17
burse 206
butterflies 15, 66, 86–7, 92, 215
Byzantium 200, 224

**C**

Calder, Alexander 161
calligraphy 9, 168–9
Cambay 60
Canada 199, 245
Capey, Reco 15, 25
carpets and rugs
  British/English 23, 35, 45, 153, 154, 165
  Caucasian 23
  French 229
  Indian 63, 69, 240
  Norwegian 136
  Oriental 122–3
  Persian 23, 122–3, 126, 137, 168, 217
  Turkmenistan 135
cartoons 247
cartouches 247
casement cloth 247
caterpillars 82, 84, 85
Causasia 23
Celtic designs
  influences 9, 47
  knots 247
Century Guild 97, 207
chalice veils 37
Chareau, Pierre 179
*charkhana sangi* 188
checks 188, 190–1
  buffalo 246–7
  dog's tooth 247
  Glen Urquhart 201
chevrons 128, 129, 130, 247
Chimu textiles 159
China
  abstract designs 146
  calligraphy 169
  colour 28
  conversational designs 234
  dyeing technique 25
  floral designs 81
  geometric designs 137, 143
  *hamsa* design 94
  *Hsieh-Chai* 103
  human figures 215

influence on Western design 57, 71, 247
  Taoist imagery 207
china blue 54, 247
Chinoiserie 247
chintz 247
  English 74–5
  Indian 72–3
chrysanthemums 125, 129, 142, 152
circles 142–3
  *see also* roundels
Classicism/classical
  influences 127, 166, 208–9, 223, 247
clouds 51, 125, 146
clowns 225
coats of arms 16, 240, 242–3
cockerels 102
Cocteau, Jean 222
cogs 173
Cole, Henry 61
colour and pattern 28–9
'Contemporary' 1950s style 160, 161
conversational designs 224–43
copperplate printing 14, 54
cotton 26, 247
coverage 247
Crane, Walter 211
cranes 82, 88, 94–5, 125, 133
crash 247
Craven, Shirley 163
crêpe 247
crewel-work 18, 19, 42, 70, 102, 247
crocuses 77, 81
croquis 247
Crosland, Neisha 131, 153, 165
crown 13
Crusoe, Robinson 239
Cubism 154, 231
*cyma recta* 140

**D**

daffodils 11, 58, 76
damask 12, 33, 247
Day, Lewis Foreman 14, 79, 109
Day, Lucienne 49, 111, 161

Dearle, John Henry 11, 76
delphiniums 67, 77
Devonshire Hunting Tapestries, the 232
diamond patterns 68, 136–7
diaper patterns 247
dice 170
directional patterns 247
dobby 12, 247
dogs 154, 215, 221
dog's tooth checks 247
domestic designs 170–1
Dorn, Marion 153, 155, 183, 209
'drab style' 51
dragons 97, 103, 143, 234, 235
Dresser, Christopher 105
Drummond, John 99
Ducharne, François 67
ducks 92
duplex printing 55
dyeing techniques 24–5
   batik 231, 246
   ikat 24, 25, 147, 248
   kasuri 130, 133, 192
   mordants 24, 248–9
   tie-dye 68, 130, 134, 143, 244, 250
   see also indigo
dyes, fugitive 248

E
Eastern Turkestan 186
Egypt, ancient, influence on design 154, 169, 245
Egyptian textiles 40, 50, 88, 90, 198, 208, 216
elephants 23, 37, 82, 84, 100–1
embroidered lace 20
embroidery techniques 18–19
   see also crewel-work
England
   abstract designs 147, 151, 153, 155, 160, 161, 163, 164, 165
   altar frontal 36
   Calthorpe purse 37
   carpets 23, 45, 153, 154, 165

chintz 74–5
conversational designs 225, 226, 228, 229, 230, 231, 233, 235, 236, 237, 238, 239, 241, 242, 243
dyeing technique 25
fauna 82, 83, 84, 85, 86, 87, 91, 92, 93, 95, 96, 97, 99, 102, 103
field flowers/grasses 54, 55
floral designs 11, 39, 58, 59, 61, 64, 66, 67, 68, 69, 70, 71, 76, 77, 78–9, 81
fruit designs 53
geometric designs 127, 130, 131, 133, 135, 137, 139, 140, 141, 143, 145
grids & stripes 187, 189, 193, 194, 195, 199
human figures 204, 206, 207, 208, 209, 210–11, 215, 218, 219, 223
lace 86, 121
leaves 39, 42, 45, 46, 47
medieval influences 10
objects as motifs 164, 165, 167, 172, 173, 176, 177, 180, 181, 183, 226
Oxburgh Hanging 19
patchwork 148–9
printing techniques 14, 15
stylised designs 105, 107, 108, 109, 110, 112, 113, 116, 117, 121
tapestries 17
trees 49, 50, 51
epinglés 247
epitaphios 209
Erzgebirge, Saxony 21
etched (burn-out) printing 247
ethnic designs 247

F
fans 166, 170
Fauves, the 151
ferns 45, 165
Festival of Britain (1951) 27, 111, 160–1
field flowers 54–5
figurative patterns 247–8
Finland 175
fish 88, 89, 120, 159, 227
Flanders
   lace 21, 65, 121, 220
   linen panel 232
   tapestry 16
flax 248
fleurs-de-lys 32, 126, 143, 248
floral designs 58–9
   all-over pattern 60–1
   azaleas 121
   baskets 62–5
   bouquets 66–7
   chrysanthemums 125, 129, 142, 152
   crocuses 77, 81
   daffodils 11, 58, 76
   delphiniums 67, 77
   field flowers and grasses 54–5
   garlands 70–1
   honeysuckle 79
   lilac 109, 139
   naturalistic 76–7
   on patterned ground 68–9
   peonies 66, 81, 125
   poppies 8, 39, 81
   roses 66, 67, 80, 176
   stylised 80–1
   sunflowers 69
   thistles 58, 165
   tulips 45, 62, 79, 81, 106, 113
   Victorian symbolism 78
   see also chintz
flounce 53
Foley, Jennie 241
formal designs 108–9
Fortuny, Mario 46
foulard 248
Foxton, William, Ltd. 15, 26, 151

France
   abstract patterns 150, 151, 152, 154, 155, 159, 162
   calligraphy 169
   carpets 229
   colour 29
   conversational designs 35, 225, 239, 245
   damask 12, 33
   fauna 83
   floral designs 59, 64, 67, 71
   geometric designs 127
   grids & stripes 184, 185, 191, 200, 201, 203
   human figures 204, 210, 219, 222
   image robe 32
   lace 45, 65, 85
   leaves 43, 46, 47
   objects as motifs 167, 170, 172–3, 174, 175, 179
   tapestries 10
Franklin, Benjamin 239
'French provincials' 200
fruit 52–3
   grapes 52, 53, 69, 209
   pineapples 53
   pomegranates 106, 109, 122
Fry, Roger 151
fugitive dyes 248
Futurism 154

G
gardens 176–7
   see also landscapes
garlands 70–1, 248
Garrick, David: Lethe 220
Garrick, Mrs David 73
Garthwaite, Anna Maria 49, 71
geese 94
   Chinese hamsa symbol 104
geometric shapes 9, 126–45
gingham 248
'gingham shirting' 200

Glen Urquhart check 201
Godwin, Edward William 109, 147
Gothic designs 10, 78, 108, 213, 228
Graf, Edward 245
Grant, Charles 141
grapes 52, 53, 69, 211
grasses 54–5
Greece 19, 34, 102, 134, 199, 205, 207
Greek key pattern 248
grid frameworks 198–9
grids & stripes 184–203
grotesques 248
ground (of textiles) 248
guilloche 121, 248
Gujarat, India 31, 60
   Kutch 11, 19, 99, 143

H
Hackett 201
Haite, George Charles 69, 81, 117
half-drop repeats 248
Hall, Peter 163
hamsa 104
Hanlin scholar, the 213
Heals 49, 127, 145, 153, 163, 189
Hoffman, Joseph 193
Holland see Netherlands
honeysuckle 79
Honiton lace 86, 121
Horne, Herbert 207
horses 82, 98–9, 227
   see also hunting scenes
Hsieh-Chai 103
Hulse, Clarissa 77, 165
Hulton, Mary 243
human figures 204–23
human forms 203, 222–3
Hungary 245
Hunter, Eileen 93
hunting scenes 73, 98, 221, 226, 232–3

I
ikat technique 24, 25, 147, 248
image robes 32

# Index

India
architectural designs
178
carpets 63, 69, 240
chintz 72–3
conversational
designs 224, 230,
233, 237
embroidery 11, 19,
31
fauna 25, 86, 99,
100–1
floral designs 60, 71,
72–3
geometric designs
130
grids & stripes 188,
192, 193, 205
human figures 211
influence on
European design
19, 39, 42, 102,
185 see also paisley
designs
stylised designs 104,
110
trees 51, 178
see also boteh motifs;
individual regions
of India
indigo 54, 247
china blue 54, 247
indigo discharge
technique 35
Indonesia 231
insects 84–5
bees 84, 85
butterflies 15, 66,
86–7, 92, 215
caterpillars 82, 84, 85
Iran 22
see also Persia
Ireland 89, 203
island patterns 248
Italy
architectural designs
178
chalice veil 37
floral designs 38, 59,
62
geometric designs
128
lace 20, 222–3
leaves 41, 46
and Ottoman design
106

stylised designs 13,
105, 119
tapestry 17
ivy leaves 40

## J
Jacqmar Ltd. 167
Jacquard fabrics 12, 13,
117, 248
Japan
abstract designs 152
colour 29
conversational
designs 235
dyeing techniques 24
fauna 37, 83, 87, 88,
89, 91, 92, 95, 103
floral designs 68
geometric designs
129, 130, 132,
133, 134, 139,
141, 142, 143
grids & stripes 185,
190
influence on Western
design 53, 93, 109,
147
kimonos 124–5, 248
leaves 44
objects as motifs 166,
170, 171, 179
patchwork 43
stylised designs 81,
120, 121, 124–5
trees 48, 51
Jesse trees 206
Joel, Betty, Ltd. 47
Jones, Owen: Grammar
of Ornament 113

## K
kalamkari 117
Kamalia, Punjab, India
99
kantha 101
Kashani, Maqsud 168
Kashmir designs
114–15, 237
kasuri technique 130,
133, 190
kente 248
kesa 43
key pattern, Greek 248
Kiely, Orla 164
kimonos 124–5, 248
kites 227

Klee, Paul 161, 227
Knox, Archibald 47
Koi carp 88
Korea 94, 126

## L
lace
bobbin 20, 21, 86,
220–1
contemporary 165
flounce 53
French design 65
Honiton 86. 121
human figures in
220–1
Mechlin 65
techniques 20–1
Larcher, Dorothy 189
lattices 69, 192–3
see also trellis designs
Le Brocquy, Louis 203
leaves 11, 14, 40–7,
111, 164
acanthus 45, 83, 93,
103, 246
ferns 45, 165
ivy 40
maple 44
oak 40
lettering 26, 168–9,
175, 211
Liberty & Co. 55, 97
lilac 109, 139
lions 83, 118, 119, 217,
224, 232, 233
liseré 248
lobsters 89
Logan, Muckett and
Co., Manchester 95
Lotto carpets 123
lozenges see diamond
patterns
luggage 171
Lyon, June 161

## M
machines & tools 172–3
Mackintosh, Charles
Rennie 80, 140, 144
influence of 55
McLeish, Minnie 15, 87,
151

MacMurdo, A.H. 97
Madras cotton 248
Mahler, Marian 147
maple leaves 44
maps 236–7
marine life 88–9
fish 88, 89, 120, 159,
227
lobsters 89
octopus 89
Marx, Enid 131
Mary, Queen of Scots 18
Mechlin lace 65
medieval influences 10,
35, 78, 108, 109,
143, 213
see also Gothic
designs
Mexico 244
images of 245
millefleurs 248
Miró, Joan 161, 227
Modernism
designs 202–3
influence of 53, 139,
154
moiré 248
Moody, Helen Wills 227
mordants 24, 248–9
Morris, William 123,
246
carpets 23, 45
fabrics 25, 27, 35,
79, 93, 97, 109
tapestries 83, 91,
103, 211
Morris & Co. 76
mosaic designs 249
motifs, categories of
30–1, 249
Mughal designs 11, 249
multi-directional
patterns 60
mythological subjects
208–9, 234–5
beasts 102–3, 118,
119, 143
see also dragons;
unicorns

## N
Napper, Harry 59, 235
naturalistic designs
76–7, 249
Navajo designs 156–7
needlepoint 20

negative spaces 249
Netherlands, the 16, 35,
63, 83, 144, 232
Nicholson, Nancy 235
Nixon & Co. 238
noren 89
Norway 136

## O
oak leaves 40
oak trees 51
Oberkampf, Christophe-
Philippe 238
octopus 89
offset patterns 249
ogees 104, 106–7, 249
Oliver, Mary 181
ombrées 249
Omega Workshops 133,
140, 151
optical art/illusions
144–5, 184, 249
trompe-l'oeil 250
opus anglicanum
embroidery 228
ostriches 83
Ottoman designs 42, 43,
52, 64, 65, 105, 106,
116, 119, 179, 212,
241
outline quilting 249
Oxburgh hanging, the
18

## P
painterly designs 150–1
paisley designs 13,
116–17, 249
Pakistan 31, 99, 129,
191
palampores 51, 56, 86,
224
Palmer, Sue 183
paper garments 33
Parker, Mary 148
pastoral subjects
210–13
patchwork 148–9
Japanese kesa 43
peacocks 81, 82, 96–7,
103, 122
pelican 138
peonies 66, 81, 125
Persia
carpets 23, 122–3,
126, 137, 168, 217

fabrics 118, 138, 188, 211, 214, 217, 222, 240
  *see also* Iran
Peru 158–9
pictorial scenes 228–31
pillow lace *see* bobbin lace
pine trees 51, 125, 133
pineapples 53
plaids 200–1
  *see also* tartan
plain weaves 12
playing cards 170
Poiret, Paul 154, 196
Politowicz, Kay 15
polygons 134–5
pomegranates 106, 109, 122
poppies 8, 39, 81
pre-Columbian designs 158–9
Priestley, Sylvia 39
printing techniques 14–15
  block 14, 246
  burn-out (etched) 247
  copperplate 14, 54
  duplex 55
  resist (reserve) 249
  roller 14, 55, 249
  screenprinting 14, 39, 249–50
  table 250
psychedelic designs 145, 162–3
Pugin, A.W.N. 26, 35, 78, 105, 108, 113, 143

**Q**
quails 90
quatrefoils 126, 249
quilting, outline 249

**R**
rabbits 82, 83
Radford, Emma 86
railroading technique 249
Rajasthan, India 110, 130
Reeves, Ruth 231, 233
religious subjects 16, 17, 208–9, 226, 227

angels 207, 220
Renaissance influences 62, 63, 105, 107, 112, 113, 249
repeats 14, 249
  half-drop 248
  large 112–13
  small 110–11
resist (reserve) printing 249
Rhodes, Zandra 11
ribbon designs 70–1, 125
Robert Jones & Co. 96
rococo designs 19, 21, 49, 64, 71, 249
roller printing 14, 55, 249
Roman stripes 249
Rorschach, Hermann: ink blot tests 113
roses 66, 67, 80, 176
rosettes 118–21
roundels 104, 118–21
  human figures in 218–19
  *see also* circles
rugs *see* carpets and rugs
Russia 234

**S**
sailors 33
St. Edmundsbury Weavers 131
Sampe, Astrid 189
sample books 12
samplers 37
Sanderson, Arthur, & Sons 77
*sarasa* 185
scale 249
scissors motifs 173
Scotland
  lace 165
  tartan 9, 194, 195, 197
  textiles 49, 80, 85, 140, 144, 219
screenprinting 14, 39, 249–50
screw-eyes 173
scrolls 104
Selby, Margo 165
*senmurv* 118
*serasers* 119

'setts' (of tartans) 197
Sheldon workshops 17, 98, 208, 236, 243
shells 64
shiboru 250
side repeat designs 250
silk 26
Silver Studios 47, 79, 97, 241
simple weaves 12
Skane region, Sweden 135
Slade, S.M. 161
*soumak* 138
South America 154, 158–9
space travel 182–3
Spain 37, 126, 168
spandrels 250
*sperveri* 19
spinning tops 174
spiral designs 152–3
Spitalfields, London 42
sporting motifs 226–7
  hunting scenes 73, 174, 211, 232–3
square repeat designs 250
squares 132–3
Squires, Eddie 163
squirrels 83
Steichen, Edward 171
Straub, Marianne 139, 160, 161
strawberries 25, 46, 93, 176
*strié designs* 250
stripes
  balanced 246
  combinations 188–9
  Roman 249
  simple 190–1
stylised designs 104–25
sunflowers 69
swallows 93
Sweden 135, 189, 217, 230
*Syringa vulgaris* 139

**T**
tabards 33
tabby 12, 250
table printing 250
Talbert, Bruce J 53
Tamil Nadu 193
Taoist imagery 207

tapestry weaves 16–17
tartan 9, 194–7
  'setts' 197
  *see also* plaids
tennis motifs 175
thistles 58, 165
thrushes 25, 93
ticking 187
tie-dye 250
Timney Fowler Ltd. 181, 223
Timorous Beasties 85, 113, 219
toiles 218–19
  figures in 238–9
tool motifs 172–3
Topolksi, Felix 39
*torchon* lace 21
tortoises 125, 133
Tournai tapestry, the 17
Townsend, Charles Harrison 113
toys 174–5
trains 174
Transylvania 22
Tree of Jesse 208
Tree of Life 56–7, 97, 122
trees 31, 48–51
  oak 51
  pine 51, 125, 133
  willows 79
trellis designs 69, 138–9
Trevelyan, Julian 231
trompe-l'oeil 250
tulips 45, 62, 79, 81, 106, 113
Tunisia 185
Turkey 29, 30, 106, 107, 123, 177
  Iznik potteries 109
  Ottoman designs 42, 43, 52, 64, 65, 105, 106, 116, 119, 179, 212, 241
Turkmenistan 135
turnover patterns 250
tweeds 200–1
twill 250

**U**
umbrellas 171, 205
unicorns 235
USA
  abstract designs 147

conversational designs 231, 233, 237, 245
fruit 53
grids & stripes 185, 197
human figures 205
Navajo designs 156–7
objects as motifs 171, 182, 227
Uzbekistan 147

**V**
Venetian motifs 35
Victoria, Queen 195, 196
volutes 250
Voysey, C.F.A. 39, 46, 49, 213, 225, 241

**W**
Walton, Allan, Textiles 133, 141
Warner textiles 163, 183
warp 250
warp prints 250
Washington, George 239
watch parts 173
Waters, Daniel, & Sons 13
Watteau, Antoine 217
wave forms 140–1, 184
Wealleans, Jane 223
weaving techniques 12–13
Webb, Philip 83, 93
weft 250
Westwood, Vivienne 201
wheel motifs 19, 44
Wiener Werkstätte 87, 193, 202
willows 79
Wilson, Scottie 187
wool 26

**Y**
yarn 26–7
yarn-dyed textiles 250
*yuzen* 44, 48, 51, 83, 124, 141, 250

**Z**
zigzags 95, 128–31, 157

# Acknowledgements

**AUTHOR ACKNOWLEDGEMENTS**

I would like to thank Jason Hook for making this work possible in the first place, and my editor Sanaz Nazemi, who made the whole compilation process an enjoyable and rewarding one; Elaine Lucas at the Victoria and Albert Museum for her valiant efforts in picture research; and Katie Greenwood for all her hard work and support. My colleague Kerry Walton has helped the project with her expertise in contemporary textiles. Finally, I would like to thank Lynne Edwards for her all-round efforts to assist me and the project.

**PUBLISHER ACKNOWLEDGEMENTS**

Ivy Press would like to thank the Design Library: *Textile Designs, Two Hundred Years of European and American Patterns* by Susan Meller and Joost Elffers, Abrams, New York 1991 (*Textile Designs Digital*, the royalty-free CD ROM version of this book is available from the Design Library www.design-library.com); the Musées des Tissus et des Arts Décoratifs, 34 rue de la Charité, F-69002 Lyon, www.musee-des-tissus.com; the Royal Ontario Museum; and Simon Seivewright, for their support. Special thanks go to the Victoria and Albert Museum and V&A Images for their assistance with this publication.

The publisher would like to thank the following individuals and organisations for their kind permission to reproduce the images in this book. Every effort has been made to acknowledge the pictures, however we apologise if there are any unintentional omissions.

**PICTURE CREDITS**

All images courtesy of and © V&A Images, Victoria and Albert Museum except for the following:

Art Archive/Archaeological Museum Lima: 159 (top left). Bridgeman Art Library: 203 (bottom right), Louis le Brocquy, 'Flight', 1955. Screen-printed linen, © The artist. Neisha Crosland: 77 (bottom right), 131 (bottom), 153 (bottom right), 165 (bottom right), 187 (bottom right). Design Library: 147 (bottom left), 151 (bottom left), 152 (right), 154 (left), 159 (bottom), 162, 167 (right), 169 (top right), 170 (right), 172, 173 (top left), 174, 175 (top), 182, 184, 185 (top right), 191 (top, bottom left), 197 (bottom left), 200, 201 (top left), 203 (top left, top right, bottom left), 225 (bottom left), 226 (top left, bottom left), 245 (top left, bottom right). Dover Books: 197 (top left, top right). Clarissa Hulse: 77 (bottom left), 165 (top right). Orla Kiely: 164. Marimekko: 175 (right). Musées des Tissus et des Arts Décoratifs: 173 (top right, bottom left, bottom right), photo by Pierre Verrier. Osterley Park and House, The National Trust: 60 (bottom right). Royal Ontario Museum © ROM: 156–7, 158 (left), 199 (right), 202, 222 (left), 244, 245 (top right, bottom left). Margo Selby: 165 (top left). Timorous Beasties: 85 (bottom right), 113 (bottom right), 165 (bottom left), 219 (bottom right). Sue Timney and Timney Fowler Fabrics: 181 (right), 223 (bottom right).